WILLIAM CAXTON

The First English Editor

Caxton: reputedly from an early portrait, but unauthenticated. (*Radio Times*)

A BIOGRAPHY OF

William Caxton

The First English Editor
PRINTER, MERCHANT AND TRANSLATOR

Richard Deacon

FREDERICK MULLER LIMITED

First published in Great Britain 1976 by
Frederick Muller Limited, London NW2 6LE
Copyright (©) 1976 Richard Deacon

ISBN 0 584 10022 1

Printed and bound in Great Britain
by W & J Mackay Limited, Chatham

Contents

Illustrations

I

Man of Kent or A Kentish Man?

I<small>T</small> might have been easier to have established William Caxton's birthplace if there had not been that centuries' old rivalry between the "Men of Kent" and "Kentishmen".

Those born to the east of the River Medway are called "Men of Kent", while those born on the left bank are "Kentishmen". This tradition is said to date back to the first Kentish settlements, the area to the east being colonised by the Goths and that on the west of the river by Frisians.

Needless to say both the "Men of Kent" and the "Kentishmen" claim William Caxton as one of them. Unfortunately Caxton himself was imprecise on the subject. In the preface of his first book printed in the English language, *The Histories of Troy*, he states: "I was born and lerned myn englissh in Kente in the weeld where I doubte not is spoken as brode and rude englissh as is in ony place of englond."[1]

At the time Caxton wrote it would not be unusual to fail to pin-point the exact place of his birth, if such a place was then small and insignificant. Outside the large towns of Kent it would be difficult to be specific about any of the many hamlets that existed in the Weald, which extended from somewhere in the vicinity of Hever Castle in the north-west down through what is now the hop-garden area of Paddock Wood through Biddenden, Tenterden and Smallhythe to the edge of Romney Marsh in the south-east. Somewhere fairly close to a line drawn across this territory Caxton would have been born.

The term Weald applied to the land lying between the North Downs in Kent and the South Downs in Sussex, but was often used in a more restricted sense for the country south-west of the green-sand ridge which runs from Hythe through Ashford, Sutton Valence and Yalding to Westerham. In medieval times there was an iron industry in the Weald, especially close to the Sussex border. The whole area was noted for its fertility and was mainly devoted to mixed farming.

A great deal of evidence suggests that William Caxton was born at, or somewhere near, Tenterden, once called the capital of the Weald. It is today still a small, picturesque country town with some fine old buildings in its broad, green-swarded High Street, but until recently it was also an ancient borough which had Cinque Port privileges since Henry VI's reign, as the sea in those days came up as far as Smallhythe, a few miles distance away.

The name Caxton was normally pronounced Cauxton, and it was spelt in a variety of ways. About the time that William Caxton was born in the early years of the fifteenth century, there lived in Tenterden one Thomas Kaxton, a shrewd lawyer and business man. It is possible that he was William Caxton's brother, or a near relation. Thomas Kaxton became Town Clerk and later Bailiff of Lydd before eventually being appointed Town Clerk of Sandwich. In the Chamberlain's accounts for Lydd in 1458 Thomas Kaxton is mentioned as "a leading lawman" for the town of Tenterden during his transactions with the town of Rye. The Chamberlain's accounts of Romney also contain entries for John Cakstone and William Caustone shortly after the turn of the century in 1400. Possibly these, too, were relatives of William.

It was only during this century that Tenterden came to be accepted as Caxton's birthplace, and is so named by the *Dictionary of National Biography*, but no positive proof of this has ever been put forward. The public-house in that town known as the William Caxton was, in fact, previously named the Black Horse, remaining so until World War II.

Edward III, greatly impressed by the wealth which had been created in Flanders by the setting up of a flourishing cloth-making trade, ordered the establishment of similar businesses in England. For this purpose he selected the Weald of Kent as a site for the new industry and persuaded some eighty skilled Flemish cloth merchants and their families to settle there. It is probable that Caxton's ancestors were Flemish and he himself provides two clues to this. The first is his reference to the "brode and rude englyssh" spoken in the Weald of Kent, while in his preface to the *Eneydos* he mentioned a Kentish house-wife who understood the Flemish word "eyren", but not the English equivalent of eggs. In his own words Caxton said of one "Sheffelde", a Mercer, that he "came into an house and asked for meat, and especially he asked after eggs; and the good wife answered that she could speak no French; and the merchant was angry, for he also could speak no French, but would have had eggs, and she understood him not. And then at last, another said that he would have *eyren*, then the good wife said that she understood him well. Lo, what should a man in these days now write, *eggs* or *eyren*? Certainly it is hard to please every man, by cause of diversity and change of language."[2]

William Blades, the first serious biographer of Caxton in modern times, expressed no firm view on Caxton's birthplace, but thought that he descended from a family named Causton, who owned the manor of Caustons near Hadlow, a village outside Tonbridge and not far from the banks of the Medway. "The evidence is not strong," wrote Blades, "but there is no other locality in the Weald in which can be traced the slightest connection, either verbal or otherwise, with the family."[3]

Here Blades is being far too categorical. The evidence of the Caxtons of Tenterden and Lydd is substantial and this family lived in the Weald during Caxton's lifetime. Blades admits that: "Caxton's pedigree is quite unknown." But the Caustons had left Caustons Manor long before William Caxton was born, and the family seems then to have settled mainly in East Anglia, notably at Hadlow Hall in Essex, which name they undoubtedly brought with them from the Weald of Kent. There was a William de Caxton who was a prominent Mercer of the City of London in the fourteenth century and it has been suggested that he was William's grandfather. This, however, seems unlikely in view of William's own firm assertion that he came from the Weald of Kent. In 1474 one Oliver Causton was buried in the Church of St. Margaret, Westminster, and in 1478 somebody named William Caxton was buried there. It is possible that the last-named Caxton was the father of the printer, but this is without any corroboration.

Another claim is that William Caxton was born at Long Barn, a timber-framed house at Weald, near Sevenoaks, which the late Sir Harold Nicolson and his wife, Vita Sackville West, transformed from a tumble-down country cottage in 1915. At one time there was said to have been a plate attached to a beam in one of the bedrooms at Long Barn, stating that this was the room in which Caxton was born. But nobody knows where that plate is today, if indeed it ever existed. Mr. Nigel Nicolson, Sir Harold's son, states that the plate was never there in his time, though a postcard of Long Barn in 1915 is boldly captioned "Caxton's birthplace, Weald".

Mr. Nicolson adds: "Long Barn is a very old house. A coin dated between 1360 and 1369 was found stamped into the original clay floor, so it must have been at least fifty years old when Caxton was born. The tradition which links him with the house is based on nothing more than his statement 'I was born and learned my English in the Weald' and Long Barn is one of the oldest houses in the Weald. There is no further evidence for linking it with Long Barn. I have a press-cutting of March, 1914, from the *Sevenoaks Chronicle* which states that 'Caxton was born in 1423 and his father, who was probably a land-owner, lived at Long Barn'. But you can judge the reliability of this statement by the author's further supposition that Caxton was educated at Sevenoaks Grammar School (founded 1432), and that 'there is a local tradition that Caxton once came back to his old home and set up his clanking press in Long Barn'. I was brought up on this legend, and as a child used to lie awake at nights shivering with fear because I imagined I heard the old man at work in the room next to mine, always known to us as Caxton's room."[4]

It is fairly easy to see how the theory that Caxton was born at Weald arose: somebody at some time or other had changed the phrasing of what he had written to make it appear that he was born in the village of Weald and not in the Weald.

Though slightly more evidence concerning Caxton's life has come to light since William Blades had his biography published in 1877, it was he who supplied the solid framework on which all subsequent students of Caxton have based their own researches. But occasionally Blades was apt to make assertions based on flimsy evidence like his linking of William with the Caustons of Hadlow, and again on the subject of his birth date.

"It has generally been assumed," wrote Blades, "that 1412 was the date of his [Caxton's] birth, upon the sole ground that Caxton himself complained, in 1471, that he was growing old and weak, from which the inference has been drawn that he must then have been at least sixty years."[5]

This, Blades concluded, was a mistake. He based his deduction on the earliest volume of the Wardens' Accounts in the Archives of the Mercers' Company that William Caxton had been apprenticed to one, Robert Large, in 1438, and "would therefore have been born not later than the year 1421".

In the fifteenth century a man achieved what was known as his "civic majority" three years after he reached his legal majority at the age of twenty-one. In view of this, argued Blades, "the indenture of an apprentice was always so drawn that on the commencement of his twenty-fifth year he might issue from his apprenticeship". The theory was that Caxton was probably sixteen when he was apprenticed.

This would fix his birth date as about 1422 which has since been accepted by most authorities as the most accurate estimate. However, earlier authorities than Blades and even one modern expert on Caxton, Mr. N. F. Blake, disagree with Blades' thesis. J. P. A. Madden insists that as in his prologue to the *Recuyell* started in 1471 Caxton referred to himself as an old man, he must then have been not less than sixty and suggested that the year 1411 was the probable date of his birth. This seems somewhat doubtful, but there is nonetheless a strong argument for believing that Caxton was born rather nearer to 1416 than 1422. It is likely that his education continued after the age of fifteen in some form or other.

So the exact date of Caxton's birth is still not proven and his ancestry remains a matter of conjecture. One must accept from his own evidence the probability that he was of Flemish descent and that this was a factor in his departure for the Low Countries as a comparatively young man. It would seem likelier that he was born in the area of Tenterden rather than of Hadlow or Sevenoaks. Tenterden was not only an important centre of the Wealden wool trade—an old inn there is named the Woolpack—but its splendid church with the pinnacled tower was built with money contributed by descendants of some of the Flemish immigrants. The small town was approaching the peak of its importance about the time Caxton was born, and in 1449 was given special privileges as a limb of the royal borough of Rye and the Cinque Ports.

The towns of the Cinque Ports kept close associations with one another and the Caxtons of Tenterden were also related to several families of that name in Sandwich, another Cinque Port. Hugh Caxstan was living at Sandwich between 1429 and 1453, though it will be noted that the spelling of his name differed from that of Thomas Kaxton who eventually became Town Clerk of Sandwich.

Not far from Cranbrook, a small town only a few miles distant from Tenterden, was a place marked on early maps as "Causton Wood".

Tenterden (Kent) in the 1920s: Caxton's reputed birthplace. (*Radio Times*)

There were more Flemish cloth-weavers living in Cranbrook in the fifteenth century than in any other part of the Weald.

Henry Plomer in his biography of Caxton states that at the time Caxton was a boy: "Tenterden parish church had as its vicar a certain John Mooer or More, who was a scholar and possessed an unusually fine library . . . He would fit the part of Caxton's tutor very well." John Mooer was a fine scholar with a considerable library of manuscripts and was known to have given instruction in "Latin and divers subjects" to boys of his parish. But this particular Vicar of Tenterden was not there when Caxton was a boy: his term of office as Vicar was from 1479 to 1489, when he died. Among the books he bequeathed to the church were *Graduale*, the devotional work known as Pupilla Oculi and various theological works, while he left many of the other books in his vast library to Christchurch College [Oxford], Eton College, the monastery of St. Augustine in Canterbury and to various friends. He bequeathed Virgil's *Æneid* and other Latin works to one John Carlesse. One assumes that John Mooer must have been a fairly rich man to have afforded such a library unless, of course, he inherited it from a previous vicar. In that case young Caxton might have been instructed by an earlier vicar of Tenterden.

William Caxton made no reference in any detail to his education beyond stating in the prologue to his translated work, *Charles the Great*, that: "I am bounden to pray for my fader and moder's souls that in my youth sent me to schools, by which by the suffrance of God I get my living."[6] But nowhere did he say where he had been to school, or who taught him. In an eighteenth century pamphlet entitled *Miscellanies of Kent* there were two references to Caxton. One mentioned that the archives of the Parish of Tenterden contained a list of pupils of a fifteenth century Vicar of Tenterden, including the name of one "Will Kaxston", while the other stated that "this same Kaxston, the famous printer and himself a Kentishman, tells us that the name of the Isle of Thanet is derived from the Greek word, *thanatos*, meaning death. The earth of Thanet, says the same Kaxston, 'is poisonous to serpents and so there are no snakes in Thanet. If you take some of the soil and sprinkle it in a countrie where snakes breed, then they will wither and die' ".[7]

Some of the archives of Tenterden were destroyed in a great fire in the Town Hall in 1661, when prisoners confined there set the place alight. Nearly all the records were burnt to ashes. This is one reason why the early biographers of Caxton in the eighteenth century had so little to work on. There is, however, no reason to doubt the authenticity of *Miscellanies of Kent*, more especially as William Caxton did make reference to the Isle of Thanet in his works. His Greek and Latin may well have been learned from a Vicar of Tenterden.

Kent in Caxton's time had suffered from the Black Death of 1348, which had decimated England and left Kent with fewer people to cultivate the land. Whereas a century before Kent had been famous for its orchards, by the 1420's these were neglected and much of the Weald had been untilled. In some respects this fertile plain had become the "Black Country" of its era, and the emphasis was much more on industry and commerce than on agriculture. Timber was used as fuel for iron-smelting furnaces. Feudalism had begun to break down and many peasants had lost their small-holdings and hired themselves out as labourers. This was a trend which Caxton himself later lamented, a fact which suggests he was the son of a well-to-do tenant farmer who was also engaged in the cloth trade. If his father had been thus employed, he would almost certainly have been in close contact with the London cloth markets, which would have given him the opportunity for arranging an apprenticeship for his son.

One of the problems in tracing Caxton's ancestors is that the name was a common one in this period; it occurs not only in Kent and Essex in its various spelling forms, but also in Suffolk. In 1922 among the papers of the late Lord Winterton, who was for many years Member of Parliament for the Old Horsham and Worthing Division, a number of charters were found relating to the manor of Little Wratting in Suffolk. These revealed that about the year 1420 Little Wratting came into the possession of one Philip Caxton, who had two sons, one named William born in 1415. These charters, which were exhibited at Tenterden during the Festival of Britain celebrations in 1951, were somewhat of a contradiction to the claim then made that Caxton was a Tenterden man, for there was nothing whatsoever in these charters to link the Caxtons of Suffolk with the county of Kent. Nevertheless the Little Wratting charters were in one instance ratified by the seal of Alderman Robert Large of London, to whom Caxton was eventually apprenticed.[8]

Caxton was, according to his own statements, a good, practising Catholic and deeply religious, possibly in a more romantic and sentimental vein than most of the English. For this reason alone he may well have been selected by a discerning clergyman for special attention and tuition. All education then, at least in the countryside, stemmed from monasteries and priories all of which had schools, or from a scholarly priest. If a boy showed promise with reading and writing, then he was sometimes given the opportunity not merely to study Latin grammar, but to see some of the illuminated manuscripts which churches and monasteries held.

Kent was rich in some of these manuscript treasures. The Abbey Church of St. Augustine in Canterbury then had about 2,000 books, which covered the classics, mathematics and even such romances as *Guy of Warwick*, *Lancelot du Lac* and *The Story of the Graal*. There was another large library at Christchurch, Canterbury, of which Eastry's catalogue, compiled in 1331, mentions 1,850 volumes, while there was a smaller but impressive library at Dover Priory.

The early days of Caxton's education would provide a rich contrast for the boy from his home surroundings. Even a well-to-do tenant farmer of the period lived in comparatively rude comfort. There would be one main room used for work, cooking and sleeping, and a roofed-chamber above this where husband and wife would keep their most coveted possessions. The building itself might well be built of wattle, with a roof of thatch or red tiles and timber cross-beams. There would be an earth floor covered with rushes and a hole in the roof for the smoke from the fire in the centre of the main room.

To escape from this into the priest's library, or to some monastic library, to study the richly embellished manuscripts must have been like a trip into another world for a boy already fired by a thirst for knowledge and with a deep appreciation of beautiful things. It is, of course, possible that young Caxton's education might have been completed at the school attached to Christchurch Monastery in Canterbury. W. M. Cowper in an article on *Freemen of Canterbury* mentions a William Caxton, a Mercer, taking up his freedom as a citizen "by redemption" in 1431. Many other Caxtons are mentioned in the records of Canterbury in both the fourteenth and fifteenth centuries. Coincidentally one of Caxton's greatest friends in later life, William Pratt, came from Canterbury.

The Ambitious Apprentice

𝕴T is only from 24 June, 1438, that one can positively trace the progress of William Caxton. The archives of the Mercers' Company of London clearly record that "for the past year, that is since the Feast of St. John the Baptist in the sixteenth year of King Henry VI's reign" [24 June, 1438] William Caxton was apprenticed to the merchant, Robert Large.[1]

The Mercers' Company was a London livery company, of which the first record dates back to 1172. It received its charter in 1393. Etymologically speaking, a Mercer is a merchant who deals in textile fabrics and especially in velvets and silks. But in earlier centuries the term was applied, in London at least, to a dealer in small wares. Gilbert à Beckett, the father of St. Thomas, was a mercer with a shop on the site of the Mercers' Hall, north of Cheapside and east of Ironmonger Lane. Later the Mercers moved to the south side of Cheapside, between Bow Church and Friday Street, giving their locality the name of the Mercery. It was here that the Mercers sold their small wares at stalls.

With the development of the wool trade, these small traders became more ambitious, and in 1351 violent feelings of antagonism arose between the Mercers and the Lombard moneylenders, ending in assaults by the former on the latter. This marked the beginning of the transformation of the Mercers from traders in small wares to specialists in cloth. The Sumptuary Act, 37, of King Edward III's reign in 1363 shows that the Mercers then sold woollen cloth, but not silk. But by the reign of Henry VI they had become extensive and prosperous traders not only in wool, but in silks and velvets as well, and their former small-time trade had been totally handed over to the Haberdashers' Company. Clearly the Mercers would have had links with the wool manufacturers in the Kentish Weald and this would have paved the way for the apprenticeship of young Caxton.

The Mercers' Company was by this time extremely wealthy and its

members had built themselves fine town houses in the Old Jewry. It
was here that Richard Large lived. One of the richest and most
influential members of the Mercers, Large became a Warden of the
company in 1427, Sheriff of London in 1430 and Lord Mayor of
London from 1439–40. It is almost certain that Caxton's father must
have been a man of some substance and highly esteemed for his son to
have obtained an apprenticeship with so eminent a figure as Richard
Large. The Mercers' Company had been given an *inspeximus* charter by
Henry VI in 1424 at the request of Richard Whittington, that hero of
nursery lore who became Lord Mayor of London, and who had died in
1423. Whittington had also been a Mercer, and it could well have been
that Caxton was inspired to further studies by the library which the
former Lord Mayor had bequeathed to the Guildhall.[2]

In 1438, when Caxton arrived in London, Henry VI, who had come
to the throne at the age of nine months under a protectorship, was just
seventeen years old. Ten years before Richard Beauchamp, Earl of
Warwick, became Henry's governor, with full instructions as to how
the young King was to be brought up: "to draw him to virtue by ways
and means convenable . . . to teach him literature, language and
other manner of cunning". The end product was a virtuous, in some
ways saintly King, fond of learning and devoted to furthering education, but quite unworldly and never a match for his many enemies.
Ideally, Henry VI would have made a good abbot, or monk, shut away
from the world of secular affairs.

England was still constantly engaged with her traditional enemy
across the Channel, France, but there were in the country, even then,
stirrings of a renaissance of learning, which the young King did all he
could to encourage. Perhaps the most significant event of that year,
1438, as far as Caxton was concerned was not in England at all, but the
news which filtered through to London of the invention of a form of
printing by an innkeeper of Haarlem in Holland, named Laurenz
Janszoon Coster. It was news which quickly became a legend and was
then forgotten. No doubt there was something of a primitive form of
printing named "Costeriana", which had evolved, but there is little
evidence of it today. Yet young Caxton may well have heard all about
it.[3]

His education, wherever it was undertaken, must have been
thorough, for he would have had to know how to read and write in a

comprehensive manner to undertake the tasks which Robert Large set him. Clearly, his master soon regarded him as a highly promising apprentice and singled him out as likely to progress far, this much being obvious from the speed of Caxton's advancement after the death of his master and while he was still an apprentice.

The duties of an apprentice were laid down with the purpose of ensuring that he followed a course of what can best be described as a medieval form of that "muscular Christianity" so beloved of the latter day Victorians. The Mercers' apprentice was required to attend mass and hear sermons and to learn the Catechism on Sundays and Holy Days, while in his leisure time he was bound to go to Smooth-fields (Smithfield) for archery practice and drill, especially on Sundays and Holy Days. English archery laws compelled all able-bodied males under a certain rank to practise with the bow on Sundays and holidays from childhood up to the age of sixty. Thus Caxton would only be conforming to general practice, but under the terms of his apprenticeship these rules would be rigorously enforced and he would have to put in rather more archery drill than most youths. Merchants (and this would include the Mercers) were obliged to import four good bow-staves with every ton of merchandise and ten with each butt of Malmesey wine.

These laws had enabled the English not merely to set a high standard in archery, but also to develop the long-bow, the weapon that was to give them such an advantage over the much larger French armies on the continent. The long-bow had a killing range of 250 yards. An apprentice was liable to be enrolled as a member of the Militia in the event of war or serious civil disturbance. He would then march under the command of City Aldermen and Sheriffs and accompany the Lord Mayor in the latter's capacity of Chief Magistrate to help quell disorder. The apprentice was also liable to public whippings for misconduct and to public reproof and penalties imposed for breach of the rules of conduct. That a somewhat rigid code of discipline was imposed on apprentices was not altogether unreasonable in view of their youth and the tendency of some to indulge in roisterous activities. Indeed in the early part of the sixteenth century there was a serious revolt of apprentices against foreign merchants which ended in the killing of some and the burning of their houses.

But the master also had his duties to his apprentices. By the rules of his charter he was compelled to feed, clothe and act as adviser to the apprentice as well as to teach him the arts of his job. If any master failed to comply adequately with these duties, the apprentice could lodge a complaint with the Court of Aldermen.

To become an apprentice to a merchant of a City company such as the Mercers was in itself a mark of exclusivity and made the youth a privileged person. It gave him opportunities denied to most other youths and the strict rules were on the whole a fair price to pay for this. Each apprentice had to swear an oath which included a pledge of allegiance to the Sovereign, allegiance to his master and to the rules of the company, as well as a solemn promise that he would respect and guard all secrets of the company and not indulge in trade on his own account.

Caxton would have had to learn about a wide variety of tasks from packing goods and handling and weaving bales of cloth to combing and weighing of fleeces, and how to distinguish addresses, trade marks, guild signs and different textures of cloth and to fold and wrap delicate fabrics. He would also be expected to keep a watch on materials exposed to the street, to wait on the family of Alderman Large, run errands for the Alderman's household and fetch fresh water from the conduits.

It was not until a year after Caxton was apprenticed that Alderman Large became Lord Mayor of London and, as was then customary, moved to a mansion house in Old Jewry which had been granted as the residence for the Lord Mayor elect. By all accounts this was a spacious and handsome residence which had originally been a synagogue, but after the expulsion of the Jews from England had been granted to an order of Friars and later became a nobleman's house. There were at least eighteen people resident in the Large home, including the Alderman and his second wife, Johanna, four sons, two daughters, two servants and eight apprentices. Oldys, a famous antiquarian, writing in the *Biographica Britannica*, described the Large house as formerly being "the mansion-house of Robert Fitzwalter, anciently called the Jews' synagogue, at the north corner of the Old Jewry".

The earlier "shops" of the Mercers, when they dealt purely in small wares, had been hardly better than sheds, and Cheapside, where they operated, was really a market of sheds and stalls assembled around the Old Cross. When the Mercers became dealers in woollen cloths and silks, the Haberdashers took over the stalls. But the Mercers retained some of their stalls in Cheapside, for in the ballad of the *London Lickpenny*, written in the time of Henry VI, there is this narrative in verse:

> "Then to the Cheap I began me drawn,
> Where much people I saw for to stand;
> One offered me velvet, silk and lawn,
> Another he taketh me by the hand,
> 'Here is Paris thread, the finest in the land.' "[4]

That Caxton was devoted to London is evident from what he wrote in his prologue to *The Booke Callyd Cathon*: "Unto the noble ancient and renowned city, the city of London, I, William Caxton, citizen and conjury of the same . . . owe of right my service and goodwill." That this was not merely the conventional view of an older man is evident from his reference to the fact that he had known London "in my young age much more wealthy and prosperous and richer than it is at this day; and the cause is, that there is almost none that intendeth to the common weal, but only every man for his singular profit."[5]

This latter statement may have been the regret of an older man for the passing of what seemed to him to have been "better days", but it is far likelier from what we know of the history of the period that he was accurately portraying a trend. When Caxton wrote this in Richard III's reign the country had passed through all the horrors of civil war with the Wars of the Roses. In the 1420's to the 1430's London had earned for itself the name of "The White City", supposedly because it was cleaner than most large cities, and Europeans were impressed when they visited the English capital. Perhaps even William Dunbar, composing his paean of praise to the City of London somewhat later in the same century, was harking back to the past when he declared:

> "London, thou art of townes *A per se*,
> Sovereign of cities, seemliest in sight. . . .
> London, thou art the flour of Cities all."

Young apprentices coming to London for the first time in this period were also delighted with the city and Chaucer, writing some years before Caxton's term of apprenticeship, said:

> "When there any ridings were in Cheap,
> Out of the shop thither would he leap;
> And till that he had all the sight yseen,
> And danced well, he would not come again.

A picture of the walled City of London from the "Nuremberg Chronicle" of 1493.
(*Radio Times*)

It was in Cheap that most of the processions passed. A celebration of one event or another was frequently held and Cheap was, above all, the scene of some of the splendid pageants which the wealthier citizens organised. Joustings were held there. Much colour and excitement was provided to lighten the humdrum life of an apprentice. Beside the Church of St. Mary-le-Bow, a great house of stone called the Crownsilde (meaning Royal House) was built and from this the joustings, the processions and the annual march of the Watch on Midsummer Eve were viewed.

But all was not gaiety either in the London of this period, or indeed in Cheapside itself. Despite its reputation on the continent for being a clean city, much of London was then filthy, undrained and in places had narrow, garbage-filled streets that would have been a disgrace to an Arab kasbah of the same era. All the gates of the City of London were closely guarded and shut from sunset to sunrise. The heads of traitors were exposed on spears at these gates. Riots, street fights and attacks on Jews and foreigners were frequent. In the Cheap itself less edifying exhibitions than the Lord Mayor's Procession could be seen. Bakers would be drawn along it on hurdles with short-weight loaves tied around their necks, while butchers were pilloried with stinking meat burnt beneath their noses. Officialdom was certainly more vigilant in the cause of hygiene and the quality and weight of food in these medieval times than it is today. In 1392 a rule was made that applied to the selling of bread on the stalls of West Cheap. It stated that if any loaf from Stratford was found to be deficient in weight, then the whole cart-load should be confiscated. Raids were made with regularity by the officials.

Such was the atmosphere in which young Caxton worked. He would be dressed in long worsted hose with a short tunic, a flat cloth cap and wooden-soled, heavy low shoes. It was a somewhat severe and drab apparel. His meals were taken with the Large family at the lower end of a trestle table and he would be expected to remain silent unless addressed. The chief meal of the day consisted of stewed meat or fish, leeks, cabbage and solid pastries of rabbit and pork with rye bread, washed down with a horn of beer or ale. At night, when his master went visiting, Caxton walked before the party, carrying a lantern and wearing a long club around his neck. Junior apprentices slept in a loft overhanging the archway into the yard of their master's house, but their seniors fared somewhat better on bales of cloth in the house proper.

Caxton would not have been apprenticed when the boy King Henry VI came to London after being crowned King of France, but he would at least have known the best years of Henry's reign in that city before they turned to insurrection and violence in the streets of London. Certainly he must have played a role, if only a minor one, in the festivities of the Lord Mayor's pageant and procession when Alderman Large took office in the second year of his apprenticeship. The election of the new Lord Mayor in the Guildhall, the service in the adjoining Chapel of St. Faith and the procession through the City to Westminster Palace to pay tribute to the King would have given him a considerable understanding of English institutions on the highest possible level. The youth still had much to learn: Caxton not only came from the country, but from an unsophisticated home where the English as spoken by his Flemish stock parents was, as he himself described it, "rude and broad". The English were then, as indeed to a certain extent they still are, the most xenophobic people in Western Europe. Caxton was doubtless made fun of by the Cockneys of that day, for it is recorded that they teased the Flemish weavers about their accents, asking them to say "Bread and Cheese", and then roaring with laughter when they replied "*Kase und brod*". If, as seems probable, he was a sensitive youth, this may have given him a feeling of greater kinship with the foreigners who came to the City of London, where they were not allowed to stay for more than forty days without special permission.

One must assume that during this period Caxton spent much of his time studying and improving his education, and that for this reason he was far more serious and less roisterous than most apprentices. To have achieved what he did in later life Caxton must have continued his education while he was still an apprentice, though obviously he never acquired the learning of a university student. Not for him the Shrove Tuesday football, when stall and shop-keepers had to put up barricades to protect their wares, cock-fighting, or dancing around the Maypole. It was a passion for the written word which consumed Caxton and spurred his ambitions. It was this which drove him to seek out old manuscripts and to browse in libraries. He was following a trend, one of the few that had begun in Henry V's reign, and which is perhaps best explained by this entry made during that reign in the books of the Brewers' Company:

"Whereas our mother-tongue, to wit, the English language, hath in modern days begun to be honourably enlarged and adorned, for that our most excellent lord King Henry V hath in his letters missive, and divers affairs touching his own person, more willingly chosen to declare the secrets of his will; and for the better understanding of his people hath, with a diligent mind, procured the common idiom (setting aside others) to be commended by the exercise of writing; and there are many of our craft of brewers who have the knowledge of writing and reading in the said English idiom, but in others, to wit, the Latin and French, before these times used, they do not in any wise understand; for which causes, with many others, it being considered how that the greater part of the lords and trusty commons have begun to make their matters to be noted down in our mother tongue, so we also in our craft, following in some manner their steps, have decreed in future to commit to memory the needful things which concern us, as appeareth in the following."

Such secondary education as there was covered the basic essentials, and a certain amount of Latin grammar. In the fifteenth century about forty per cent of the City merchants could read some Latin, but relatively few could speak more than a smattering of French. English literature, after lagging behind for some centuries, had begun to produce a few men of outstanding ability, notably John Gower (1330–1408), a poet of some distinction; Geoffrey Chaucer (1340–1400) and, on a lower but quite influential level, John Lydgate. Caxton was influenced by all these men and especially by his reading of Chaucer. Something of this early enthusiasm and respect for Chaucer is evident in Caxton's preface to the second edition of his printing of the *Canterbury Tales*: "Great thanks, laud and honour ought to be given unto the clerks, poets and historiographs that have written many noble books of wisdom of the lives, passions and miracles of holy saints, of histories, of noble and famous acts, . . . and of the chronicles sith [since] the beginning of the creation of the world unto this present time. . . . Amongst whom, and especial before all other, we ought to give a singular laud unto that noble and great philosopher Geoffrey Chaucer, the which, for his ornate writing in our tongue, may well have the name of a laureate poet."[6]

Caxton, ever mindful of the rude speech of the Weald, added that Chaucer had, by his labour, "made fair our English", which previously had been "rude speech and incongrue [incongruous] as yet it appeareth by old books, which at this day ought not to have place, nor be compared among nor to his beauteous volumes and ornate writings". Chaucer and Gower were both popular among scholars of the day, but there was also a contemporary poet who Caxton must have seen playing parts in the City of London festivals and mumming plays. This was John Lydgate, the itinerant player from Bury St. Edmund's, who wrote of himself:

"I am a monk by my profession,
Of Bury, called John Lydgate by my name,
And wear a habit of perfection,
Although my life agree not with the same."

Mumming and dumb-show acting were highly popular among apprentices, as were the mystery plays. Some of the senior apprentices often fulfilled the role of what would be known today as stage manager. Lydgate was ubiquitous in his pursuit of such activities. Educated at Oxford and afterwards in France and Italy, he became a prolific poet, his chief works being *The Temple of Glass*, *The Tale of Troy* and *The Complaint of the Black Knight*. Sir A. W. Ward said of him: "Though a monk, he was no stay-at-home . . . like him of the *Canterbury Tales*, we may suppose Lydgate to have scorned the maxim that a monk out of a cloister is like a fish out of water; and doubtless many days which he could spare from the instruction of youth at Bury St. Edmund's were spent among the London streets, of the sights and sounds of which he has left so vivacious a record—a kind of farcical supplement to the Prologue of the *Canterbury Tales*."

It was this record of contemporary London which captured Caxton's imagination. Not only did Lydgate write of the merchants of "the Cheap", but his *London Lickpenny* was a superb picture of the Metropolis in medieval times, though always depicting Lydgate's own lack of money. Thus . . .

"Then forth I went by London stone,
Throughout all the Canwick Street;
Drapers much cloth me offered anon;
Then comes me one cried 'Hot sheep's feet'.
One cried 'mackerel'. 'Riches green' another gan greet;
One bade me buy a hood to cover my head;
But for want of money I might not be sped."

Lydgate was a man of the world as well as a monk. If a masque was to be presented to the King, or a May game for the sheriffs and aldermen was required; a carol for some special event, a mumming play before the Lord Mayor, or a Procession for Corpus Christi, Lydgate was usually consulted and often asked to provide the poetry. He, like other scribes of his day, depended upon wealthy patrons. An illuminated drawing in one of Lydgate's manuscripts in the British Museum, shows him presenting a book to the Earl of Salisbury. Such a work would be written by hand at the command of a nobleman who would reward the author with some rich gift. This would be all he would get for his efforts unless some other scribe agreed to make further copies of the work, in which case he might have had some small extra token payments.

It was, however, the minstrels who brought to the people, including Caxton, the poems of Chaucer, Gower and Lydgate. This was clearly the intention of Chaucer and, indeed, of Lydgate. The minstrels were not perhaps eager students of the English language and all its nuances, but they were the chief medium for spreading the growing native culture, and until the invention of printing were almost entirely responsible for preserving and popularising much of Britain's early literature which otherwise could easily have been lost.

But Caxton was sufficiently ambitious to wish to penetrate the barrier between the minstrels' English and that of the libraries. He would need not merely to be ambitious, but to overcome all obstacles to his pursuit of knowledge and, above all, to seek some escape to the continent where learning could be acquired more easily. For in his early days the hand-written book or manuscript work was still rare in England, confined to the few, and not easily obtained or even borrowed. There was no drama other than the mumming and mystery plays, and poetry depended on the minstrels. The preachers did not attempt serious or well constructed sermons because in most instances they had a contempt for their largely illiterate flocks. Many merchants (and this applied especially to the Mercers) dabbled in a trade in books and rare manuscripts. Often they were asked by nobles to acquire such works from the continent and sometimes these books would be brought to England by Flemish merchants visiting the City of London. Caxton must not only have learned all about this traffic, but profited from it.

The poet John Gower was buried in Southwark Cathedral where his monument is of special interest. He is represented as lying on his back, with his hands joined in prayer and his head resting on the three books for which he was best known—*Confessio Amantis* (Confession of a Lover), *Speculum Meditantis* (Beholding Yourself in a Glass), and *Vox Clamantis* (The Voice of One that Crieth). There is a garland of roses at his head and at his feet a lion couchant. Gower died in 1409 and his works were still appreciated in Caxton's youth. That Caxton was influenced by him is clear from the fact that the *Confessio Amantis* was not only printed by Caxton in 1483, but is said to have been the most extensively circulated of all books that came from his press. Perhaps the title was as attractive to people in the fifteenth century as it would be today. The poem itself consisted of stories that were probably common to most countries of Europe and ran to thousands of lines with an easy fluency. It was written in English, at the command of King Richard II, though many of his poems were in French. Gower provided some indications of the choice of reading favoured in those days in the following verse:

> "Full oft time it falleth so,
> Mine ear with a good pittance
> Is fed of reading of romance,
> Of Idoyne and of Amadas,
> That whilom [formerly] weren [were] in my case
> And eke of other many a score,
> That loveden [loved] long ere I was bore [born]."

Caxton was constantly aware of the shortcomings of his English, for he made more than one reference to his "rude work" and "rude Englyssh", while praising the style of French writing and the ornateness of its style, sometimes to the detriment of English prose. He understood French very well indeed, speaking and writing it freely. Probably he was more at ease with the French language—certainly this was true from about 1465 onwards—than with English. The truth was that Caxton was not only critical of his own grasp of English, but he had grave doubts about his native tongue as an adequate vehicle for expressing ideas and describing events. In the time of Edward III boys in English grammar schools were not taught English, for it had been the deliberate policy of the Norman kings, carried on by their successors, to get rid of the old Saxon language and to familiarise the people with Norman French. Ralph Higden wrote that in this period: "gentlemen be taught for to speak French from the time that they rocked in their cradle, and uplandish men [countrymen] will liken themselves to gentlemen and delight with great business for to speak French."

Just before Caxton started his education this system had changed. John Trevisa, the translator of Higden, stated in 1385 that: "Sir John

Cornewaile, a master of grammar, changed the teaching in grammar-schools and construction in French . . . wherein they have advantage one way—that is, that they learn sooner their grammar, and, in another, disadvantage, for now they learn no French, which is a hurt for them that shall pass the sea." Caxton must have suffered to some extent from this system, but he overcame it sufficiently to be highly proficient in French at an early age. This could only have come about through studying in his own spare time, and through meeting with foreigners in the City of London. He had been born into an era of rapid change in the English language which varied constantly through the introduction of new words and phrases throughout his lifetime.

Something of the integrity of his outlook on translation, or his innermost doubts as to his own ability and the problems he wrestled with when turning French into good English are expressed in his preamble to *The Life of Charles the Great*: "I have emprised and concluded in myself to reduce [translate] this said book into our English, as all along and plainly ye may read, hear and see, in this book here following. Beseeching all them that shall find fault in the same to correct and amend it and also to pardon me of the rude and simple reducing. And though so be there no gay terms, nor subtle nor new eloquence, yet I hope that it shall be understood, and to that intent I have specially reduced it after the simple cunning [learning] that God hath lent me."[7]

There is another example of how Caxton had gradually grown apart from his native language over the years and which reflected the change in the mode of teaching in the schools. Towards the end of his life he referred to the fact that "some gentlemen, which late blamed me, saying that in my translations I had over curious terms, which could not be understood of common people, and desired me to use old and homely terms in my translations. And fain would I satisfy every man; and so to do, took an old book and read therein; and certainly the English was so rude and broad that I could not well understand it. And also my lord Abbot of Westminster did show to me late certain evidences written in old English, for to reduce it into our English now used, and certainly it was written in such wise that it was more like to Dutch than to English; I could not reduce nor bring it to be understood. And certainly our language now used varieth far from that which was used and spoken when I was born; for we Englishmen be born under the domination of the moon, which is never steadfast, but ever wavering, waxing one season, and waneth and decreaseth another season; and that common English that is spoken in one shire varieth from another."

Quite early on Caxton must have realised that a revolution in the use of English was slowly building up and that the old, alliterative style in poetry and prose was passing, while inspiration for creating a new mode of expression was sought on the continent. The translators of the reign of Henry VI were themselves helping to forge a new English style, being influenced by the alliterative prose of the past, while borrowing from abroad.

How soon Caxton began to study English history one does not know, but his early reading of it undoubtedly included that most popular of fifteenth century works, the *Cronicle of Brute*, which later he translated, and added to, in his work, *The Chronicles of England*, printed in 1480. Caxton himself could never be called an historian even by fifteenth century standards, but he followed the custom of his time by adding his own amendments, thoughts or details of what he had personally experienced when translating history. In *The Chronicles of England*, which began at pre-Roman times, he moulded the legends of the past with documented history and some contemporary contributions of his own into a continuous narrative, borrowing from *The History of Nennius*, the works of Geoffrey of Monmouth and Douglas of Glastonbury in the process. When it came to the interpretation of contemporary history, Caxton relied to some extent on what he had seen for himself, and, as will be seen, at times he was inhibited into an untypical brevity.

He had seen much at first hand, even as a young man. The year after he became an apprentice the rivalry between Henry Beaufort, Bishop of Winchester and Duke Humphrey of Gloucester came to a head. The Bishop of Winchester led the party in favour of peace between England and France, and Gloucester headed the pro-war faction. This quarrel dated back to the time when Gloucester, freed from his marriage to Jacqueline, Countess of Hainault and Holland, by a papal decree, scandalised many by marrying Eleanor Cobham, Jacqueline's lady-in-waiting. The Bishop of Winchester and his family retaliated by accusing the Duchess of practising witchcraft on the young King.

Gloucester's authority was undermined by the revelations of his wife's dabblings in sorcery: she had consulted the Witch of Eye in Suffolk. The Duchess sought sanctuary in Westminster Abbey, but this was refused. She was imprisoned in the Tower of London, where

she was forced to name the wizards and necromancers who were supposed to have instructed her. They were all burnt or hanged. The
Duchess herself was then forced to perform public penance by walking
barefoot through the streets of London, carrying a lighted taper and
robed in a white sheet with a scarlet "S" for sorceress woven on the
front and back. This she did for three consecutive days, walking from
the Tower to St. Paul's Cross, where a sermon was preached condemn-
ing her "crime".

This affair must have made a deep impression on young Caxton for
he narrated it long afterwards at considerable length. Verses were
composed about the Duchess's walk through the City of London, one
of these being:

> "All woman that in this world are wrought,
> By me they may ensample take:
> For I that was brought up of nought
> A prince me chose to be his make [mate] . . ."

Caxton was a diligent observer and at times had an almost journalistic
gift of brevity, though this was possibly caused as much by discretion,
when referring to topical events, as anything else. His description of
the Battle of Towton in *The Chronicles of England* is tersely written: "On
Palm Sunday after he [Edward IV], had a great battle in the north
country at a place called Towton, not far from York, where, with the
help of God, he got the field and had the victory: where were slain of
his adversaries XXV thousand men and more, as it was said by men
that were there."

He made it quite clear that he was describing something he himself
had not seen, though one would have thought that with the advantage
of verbal accounts, even third-hand, of so decisive and important a
battle, he could have found more to say. Perhaps the horror of involving
himself in the Yorkist–Lancastrian dispute was a factor.

One must remember that Caxton had no dictionaries to which he
could refer, nor had he even an English language of such power and
embellishments, such imagery and elasticity as Shakespeare was able to
profit from more than a century later. What English there was still
consisted of innumerable dialects which had little in common with one
another. He was a much perplexed student of the alchemy of words and
constantly aware of the limitations of such English language as then

existed. The Bible then was little known outside the innermost circles of the clergy. To be found in possession of a Bible without a license was regarded by the Church authorities as evidence of heresy. Lollardism, the anti-Rome movement of followers of Wycliffe, had been driven underground where it withered without learning or leadership. The only native literature which would have been accessible to Caxton would have been the works of Chaucer, Gower and Lydgate and re-productions of Mandeville's *Travels*. For the most part Caxton would have had to depend not on the written, but the spoken English word as expounded by the minstrels in ballads, by the itinerant players and by men and women who practised the social art of story-telling.

In arriving at an approximate date for Caxton's apprenticeship to Robert Large there are other considerations to be taken into account. N. F. Blake writes: "that Robert Large paid the two-shilling fee for his apprentice William Caxton in 1438 is no guarantee that Caxton actually started his apprenticeship in that year. The Account Book is, as its name implies, a record of payments to and by the company; it is not a record of when apprentices were enrolled or issued . . . Con-sequently although Caxton had started his apprenticeship by 1438, it is not necessary to assume that he became an apprentice in that year."[8]

It is true that on average apprenticeships lasted from seven to ten years, but a careful assessment of the records of the Mercers' Company shows that the length of service of an apprentice lasted from seven to fifteen years and that the longer period of service was by no means unusual.

3

Appointment in Bruges

CAXTON had only been apprenticed to Robert Large for three years when the latter died. Large's will reveals that he owned the manor of Horham in Essex, which fact may have caused William Blades to have linked Caxton with the Essex Caustons. There is no indication in this will of any family association of the Larges with the county of Kent. Large died on 24 April, 1441, just thirteen days after he made his will and in which he left substantial sums of money: to his parish church of St. Olave in Old Jewry, where he was buried, for the repair of London Bridge, for the completion of a new aqueduct, for poor maids' marriages and to poor householders.

His apprentices were not forgotten. Richard Bonyfaunt, Henry Okmanton, Robert Dedes, Christopher Heton and William Caxton, all of whom were entered in the Mercers' Company books as "apprentices of Robert Large", were all left bequests ranging from £50 to 20 marks, the latter being the amount given to Caxton, who appears to have been the youngest. Even 20 marks was a considerable sum for those days. Although Large's will was made a mere matter of days before he died, there is no mention in it of any arrangements for his apprentices in the event of his death. Death of a master did not release an apprentice from his indentures and it was customary to nominate a new master in a merchant's will. As this was not done, one must assume that the executors of Richard Large found a new master and a new home for Caxton, as they were bound to do by law.[1]

It is nonetheless curious that a will which went into a great deal of detail and covered the family, servants and friends of the Alderman, omitted to make any future plans for the apprentices. Possibly this had already been done verbally, but in the case of Caxton there is no evidence of a new master having been appointed for him. It is highly probable therefore that Caxton was sent abroad shortly after Robert Large's death and that he had already been marked out for advancement, possibly with a verbal promise, during the last months of the Alderman's life.

Large had extensive business with the Low Countries and especially with Bruges, which at that time was the centre of English trade overseas. During his apprenticeship Caxton probably obtained a good deal of knowledge of foreign trade and he would, of course, frequently meet other merchants from the continent. As part of an apprentice's training —especially if he was an apt pupil—it was not uncommon for one to be sent abroad. The Rev. John Lewis, who wrote a life of Caxton in the early part of the eighteenth century, stated: "It has been guessed that he was abroad as a travelling agent or factor for the Company of Mercers and employed by them in the business of merchandise."[2]

The best indication that this deduction is correct, is to be found in Caxton's own statement that in 1471 he had "contynued by the space of XXX yere for the most parte in the centres of Brabant, Flanders, Holand and Zeeland".[3] This should not be interpreted, as Blades was apt to do, that Caxton spent his entire time on the continent. It is known for certain that he returned home at least once during this period. It is probable that he made several other visits.

There were seven apprentices of Large, each of whom would have been expected to stay for seven years. Some have suggested that Caxton's indentures were cancelled, but again this is purely supposition and seems most unlikely, especially as no reference was made to this in Large's will. On the other hand he may well have been given leave of absence from his apprenticeship for some special assignment for the Mercers' Company in Bruges. If Caxton's own calculation of thirty years spent in the Low Countries is accurate and not just an approximate one, then he must have left London for the continent, and most likely for Bruges, within a few months of Large's death. The money he received from Large would, by modern standards (and as these are changing so rapidly it is not easy to be accurate) be worth about £200, though this is perhaps hardly a fair comparison. It would be just enough for an ambitious young man to take a chance of making good in a foreign country, though undoubtedly that would have been a gamble. Yet a gamble of sorts is possibly what it was, reinforced perhaps by a very modest assignment for the Mercers. For in this very period that Caxton describes himself as spending in Brabant, Holland and Zeeland, there was a ban on commercial enterprise between

King Henry VI, saintly and studious. (*Radio Times*)

England and the Duchy of Burgundy, to which these three territories belonged. This ban lasted for twenty of the thirty years Caxton mentioned. No English goods were allowed to pass to the continent except through the port of Calais and Caxton himself declared later "in France I never was".

In the early years of Henry VI's reign the understanding which England had achieved with the Duchy of Burgundy continued and was nurtured and encouraged by the Duke of Bedford, who, by reason of this alliance, had completed the conquest of Maine and Anjou. But in 1432, when the war in France was not going well and the Burgundians were thinking of withdrawing from it, Bedford, whose wife had died, married Jacqueline of Luxemburg, a member of the House of Burgundy. By doing this Bedford hoped to bolster the Anglo–Burgundian alliance, but his plan badly misfired. The Luxemburg section of the House of Burgundy omitted to consult the Duke Philip of Burgundy prior to the marriage and he took umbrage. The French drove a further wedge between England and Burgundy and the situation was worsened after the death of Bedford in 1435. Burgundy deserted from the English cause. It is said that Henry VI wept when he heard the news.

Thus it does seem possible, if not indeed probable, that Caxton came to some kind of an arrangement with the Mercers' Company to fend for himself on the continent and to try to do what business he could on their behalf, some of it undoubtedly of a secretive nature in attempts to circumvent the trade prohibitions. In short, he would be a freelance agent, trying to find ways and means of getting around the commercial laws which would not allow people to trade in their own ways. Charles Knight opined that: "William Caxton was in truth an accredited smuggler for law-makers who attempted to limit the wants and the means of satisfying the wants of the people they governed in deference to the prejudice of those who thought that trade could only exist under a system of the most stringent prohibition."[4]

Restrictions were practised on all sides. At one time the Duke of Burgundy issued an edict banning the import of English cloths. A Statute of King Henry VI, in 1429, stated that the price of wool and tin sold at Calais should "not be abated, but augmented and put to greater increase and advantage", and for "the whole payment to be made in hand". It soon became obvious that such legislation enacted in a spirit of spite and greed would not work, for shortly afterwards it was discovered that the English merchants "have not sold, or cannot sell, nor utter their cloths to merchants aliens, whereby the King has lost his customs". A concession was thereupon made: the merchants were permitted to sell for six months' credit.

Year after year the law continued to insist that: "all wools, woolfells, hides, lead and tin and divers other merchandise passing out of the realm of England, the lands of Ireland, Wales and Berwick-upon-

Tweed, ought to repair to the staple at Calais and to none other place beyond the sea."

The same Statute that enacted this conceded in its preamble that: "a great substance of the merchandise which ought to repair to the said staple do repair into Flanders, Holland, Zeeland and Brabant, without custom or charge; and moreover, the same wools and merchandises be sold in the same parts at so low a price that the merchants aliens be so greatly enstored of the same, that they come not to Calais to buy their merchandises."

Thus it is not difficult to see what might be the reasons for Caxton setting off for the Low Countries in 1441. The restrictive legislation did not deter enterprising merchants from trying to get around the law. By Henry VI's reign Calais had fallen into a state of commercial decay. Edward III had ordered that all merchandise should be offered at Calais, which he had captured for the English in 1347. Large sums in revenue accrued to him as a result of this, sometimes to the extent of £68,000 a year. By Henry VI's reign, however, the revenues had declined to a mere £12,000 annually, mainly because the wool had been sold in Brabant and elsewhere.

The City of Bruges was the seat of government of the Dukes of Burgundy and also the trading centre for all territories in this area. Merchants from all parts of Europe flocked there. After Bremen and Lubeck it was the most important town in the Hanseatic League and as a port it rivalled Hamburg. The League, which was originally an association of North German trading towns, had existed since the twelfth century. In the middle of the fourteenth century it had developed into a kind of medieval Common Market, the control passing from the merchants to the civic administrators of the various towns. Delegates were sent from each town to Assembly meetings of the League; however, these meetings were often held at intervals as long as eighteen months and there were deficiencies in the administrative machinery of the League. Its real strength tended to remain in the hands of the merchants. From the twelfth to the sixteenth century Bruges was the largest commercial city in the north of Europe, a centre for the English and Scandinavian trade as well as the emporium of Hanseatic, Venetian and other Italian merchants. Its citizens had played a prominent part in the bloody "Flemish Vespers" and the succeeding defeat of the French at Courtrai in 1302. The tapestries and cloths of

Bruges were famous throughout Europe and its cloth-workers' guild was very important. At the height of its prosperity Bruges had a population of 200,000. Yet already in the fifteenth century there were warnings of the ultimate decline of this city of bridges and canals. It was then that the silting up of the seaway to and at Sluis began and this, coupled with the growth of Antwerp, and later the discovery of America marked a gradual weakening of Bruges' commercial supremacy. Yet the spirit of independence of the citizens of Bruges remained strong and as late as 1488 this was exemplified in their holding as a prisoner for some months the Roman King (afterwards Emperor) Maximilian, and forcing him to abdicate the government of Flanders.

In Caxton's time Bruges was not merely a trading centre, but one backed by an adequate and efficient banking system that added to its status as a commercial city. Most traders of any standing had bank accounts and settled their debts by paper transactions, thus obviating all manner of exchange difficulties. The banking system, in fact, developed swiftly during the period of Caxton's residence in Bruges. First of all two parties—creditor and debtor—were required to be present when any transaction of this kind was effected. Later this was modified for convenience by substituting written instructions for physical presence and in due course a document endorsed by the payee could be made in favour of a third party. Though this was sound commercial practice, it also saved merchants from borrowing money from usurers, which was a practice firmly condemned as sinful by the Church.

The history of Western Europe had been dominated for more than a hundred years by the spasmodic and frequent outbreaks of war between England and France, into which Burgundy had on occasions been drawn, as we have seen. By and large these wars had brought prosperity to England and a good deal of ruin to France. They had also helped to bring about the emergence of Burgundy as a continental power with widespread influence of her own. It had been Philip "The Good", Duke of Burgundy, who had begun to bestow favours on the English community in Bruges. On the murder of his father, John the Fearless, in 1419, Philip vowed vengeance on the French Dauphin and sought protection from the English. It was this alliance between England and the Duchy of Burgundy which had enabled Henry V to subdue the north of France. But after Philip's relations with England cooled and he made peace with the French he still showed favours to England on occasions. For example as late as 1446 Philip conveyed special privileges on the English Merchants, or the Merchant Adventurers as they were known, despite the fact that England had discriminated against the Duchy by her insistence on all goods being offered for sale via Calais. Two years later, though, noting how English goods were pouring into his dominions, the Duke decreed that no woollen cloths at all should be allowed in.

Then, as now, there were complaints about the quality of English goods in England as much as elsewhere. A Statute of 1441 stated that: "whereas worsted was sometime a good merchandise, and greatly desired and loved in the parts beyond the sea, now because that it is a false work, and a false stuff, no man thereof taketh regard, which is great damage to the King's customs."

In those days a journey to Bruges could take some weeks, if the weather was stormy. Boats sailing from Sandwich to the Flemish coast sometimes stopped at a French port *en route*, and occasionally took as long as three weeks. Caxton always maintained close relations with the port of Sandwich—this much is clear from various transactions he made over the years—and it is probable that he sailed from Sandwich, though, according to his own account, he would not have set foot in France. On arrival in Bruges he would almost certainly enter the English community in that city, at whose head was the Governor of the English Merchants who had a handsome house with chapel attached.

The rapid growth of the cloth trade in the fourteenth century led, in England, to a large expansion of the cloth industry for the home and overseas markets in the following century. This saw the creation of the Merchant Adventurers, who gained ground at the expense of the Staplers. This was a chartered company whose Governor had control over Scottish as well as English traders in Flanders even though the Scots then still retained their independence. This was easily explained by the fact that the Scottish and English traders tended to keep together in a foreign capital and indeed the Merchant Adventurers was founded mainly for reasons of self-protection of traders. The Mercers' Company, still the largest of all City companies, took the lead in creating this organisation and there were more Mercers among the Merchant Adventurers than merchants of any other company.

The Mercers' Company can be compared in terms of power, influence and authority with that of the East India Company in Victorian

times. The great merchant companies possessed the same kind of oli-
garchical power as the trade unions today. In fact the government of
London during this era was largely conducted and controlled by the
great merchant companies, all of whom supplied the Lord Mayors and
Aldermen of the fifteenth century. They not only owned fine houses, but
splendid ships and had agents such as Caxton in Bruges and other
trading centres in Europe. Much of the intelligence obtained at the
Court came from the merchants; successive kings began to depend on
the friendships of City merchants and the Staplers actually lent money
to the government.

For the first few years of his stay in Bruges (and we cannot be sure that
he did not travel extensively during this period), there is no record of
Caxton's activities—all is surmise. Almost certainly he became a Free-
man of his Guild and completed, or was finally released from, his
apprenticeship about 1446, though no record has been kept of this,
presumably because he was out of the country. Blades seems to think
that he immediately went into business on his own account, but that is
by no means certain and it is much more likely that he was an agent for
someone in the Mercers' Company. He would, however, have profited
from the privileges conferred on the Merchant Adventurers in 1446,
for in 1449 there was some evidence that he was doing well for himself
and sufficiently in funds to be able to go surety for another merchant
for the sum of £110, a figure which can be multiplied by ten to give
some indication of its comparative value today. In the archives of
Bruges a document is preserved which states that: "William Craes, an
English merchant, complainant, and John Selle and William Caxton,
English merchants also, defendants, have this day [2 January, 1449]
appealed for justice before Roland de Vos and Guerard le Groote, our
Fellow Sheriffs. The said complainant says that John Granton, merchant
of the Staple, at Calais, was bound and indebted to him in certain sums
of money; that is to say, firstly in £60 sterling for and because of a
certain obligation, and further in the sum of £50 sterling on account
of a certain exchange which had taken place between them, as well as
for expenses and costs incurred in that matter, amounting on the whole

to £110 sterling. For this sum he had caused the said John Granton to be arrested in the town of Bruges, and that the said John being arrested, the said John Selle and William Caxton became sureties for him in equity and law."[5]

The judges found in favour of Craes and ordered Selle and Caxton to find security for the amount owing.

The next note of interest is that in 1453 Caxton paid a brief visit to England, accompanied by Richaert Burgh and Esmond Redeknape. The archives of the Mercers' Company record that these three were made Liverymen. There are certain curiosities about this visit to London. In the first place the entry indicating the admission of the three as Liverymen is deleted and underneath is written "*qz int' debitores in fine copotq.*". This would suggest that the fees were cancelled. Then again, on 11 December, 1453, Caxton went on record as assigning all his property, "both real and personal in England and beyond the seas" to Robert Cosyn, citizen and Mercer of the City of London and to John Rede of the same city. This may possibly have had some indirect connection with the Craes affair, but suggests it was an attempt to protect property from seizure.

Was Caxton already a person of such influence that he could ignore the rules of his company? In 1453 he was fined 3s. 4d. for not attending at the "riding" of the Lord Mayor, Geoffrey Fielding, who was also a Mercer. Then again about the same period there is a hint that he was an intermediary for the Duchess of Burgundy in personal deals that she was making in England. This was not the Duchess by whom later he was employed, but the wife of Philip the Good. Between 1450 and 1455 there were various entries in the accounts books of the Mercers' Company referring to transactions made by the Duchess. It is true there was no mention of Caxton in any of these entries, but as the Mercers' representative in Bruges he must have been involved. Caxton used the port of Sandwich (probably with the assistance of his relatives there) for many transactions and an item of 1451 in the Mercers' books refers to "a writ directe to Sandewyche for the gownys of the gentil womans of the duches of Burgeyn".

Caxton must have kept the closest of links with England throughout this early period of his stay in the Low Countries otherwise he would never have had the promotion he eventually secured. Possibly from his viewpoint in the Low Countries, Caxton had a keener appreciation of the political realities in England than had many more important people in London. At any rate it is significant that Caxton had acquired some influence with the House of Burgundy at the very time when they were drawing away from their previous allegiance to England. Much later there is evidence that Caxton retained his intense loyalty to England and in the long run did his utmost to obtain for her the best possible terms in trade. Meanwhile the increasing power and influence that Burgundy wielded must have given him an added advantage. Olivier de la Marche (1426–1502), a French nobleman who served the Dukes of Burgundy from Philip the Good through Charles the Bold to Duke Philip the Fair, wrote that: "peace was made at the town of Arras between King Charles of France, seventh of that name, and Duke Philip of Burgundy. The two princes showed themselves so upright in protecting their oaths, words and promises that the peace was never broken by them, nor suffered to be broken or invaded [by others]. . . . From this there came such advantage to the realm of France that the English were by that King driven out of Normandy and Guienne and never again prospered in France; and the lands of the Duke Philip, both those he held from France and those from the Empire, remained for so long in prosperity and free of war that they became the richest and most powerful realm in the world".

It was on his return to Bruges from London in 1453 that Caxton began to be increasingly important in his role as a Merchant Adventurer. Probably it was in this period that his close relationship with the Court of Burgundy began. He appears to have had control of certain revenues of the Duchy for the purchase of books and manuscripts and to have had access to its libraries. His own comment on this period was that: "oft I was excited of the venerable man, Messire Henry Bolomyer, Canon of Lausanne, for to reduce [translate] for his pleasure some historie as well in Latin and in romance as in other fashion written; that is to say, of the right, puissant, virtuous Charles the Great, King of France, Emperor of Rome, son of the great Pepin, and of his Princes and Barons, as Rowland, Oliver and other."

Caxton himself referred to Philip the Good as "the most dear Duke of Burgundy." It is not certain that Caxton was in immediate attendance upon the Court of Philip from the beginning of his mission in Bruges until the death of the Duke in 1467, but clearly he was in the confidence of the Court after the succession to the Dukedom of the eldest son of Philip, the Count of Charolois. The latter was of a totally different character from his father and was given the nickname of "Charles the Rash", later to be changed to the more respectable "Charles the Bold". Again there was a gap in the narrative of Caxton's life from about 1453 to 1463. On 16 April, 1462, the Merchant Adventurers were given a new charter, which called for "the better government of the English merchants residing in Brabant, Flanders, etc." and under its provisions made William Obray "Governor of the English Merchants" at Bruges.

Little is known about Obray, or even of the exact date of his death, but he was succeeded sometime between June, 1462, and June, 1463, by William Caxton, according to records of the Mercers' Company. Blades took the view that Obray had been appointed by the King, but that the sovereign only confirmed a recommendation of the Court of the Adventurers. It seems probable, however, that Obray held his post long before it was officially confirmed, as in 1457 it was recorded that "the Governor of the English community William Obray" ordered the English to leave Bergen-op-Zoom because they had been insulted by a local merchant who had accused an English merchant of "lying like a tailed Englishman". One wonders whether Caxton had heard of this incident because when he edited and translated *The Golden Legend*, he dealt with the legend of how St. Augustine of Canterbury was pelted with fishtails by the local inhabitants when preaching. In an earlier manuscript of this work—that of Lamberth Ms. 72—this story is applied to the district of Dorsetshire, but Caxton's version is that the incident occurred at Strood in Kent, but that: "Blessyd be to God at this day there is no suche deformitie." It may be that Caxton mistook Dorchester for Rochester, which is near Strood, or it is likelier that St. Augustine never went near Dorsetshire and that Caxton was merely correcting the story for posterity. In 1462 Obray was dismissed from his office as Governor of the English Nation on the grounds that he had accepted a bribe from the rulers of Antwerp for giving trading preferences to that town. One would think that there must have been rather more than mere bribery to cause his removal from office, because the giving of favours for preferential trading was not uncommon in this period. It was from the year 1463 that Caxton emerged from obscurity into an influential position as "Governor of the English Nation at Bruges".

Two years earlier Prince Edward had overthrown the Lancastrian forces at the Battle of Towton and had been crowned King. He swiftly showed that he preferred a Burgundian to a French alliance, but he allowed all manner of illogical and dishonest legislation to be perpetrated in his name. Thus one of his earliest Statutes decreed that: "all manner of woollen cloths made in any other region brought into this realme of England, and set to sale in any part of this realm, shall be forfeit to our Sovereign Lord the King." All this did was to encourage the production of inferior goods and to protect such fraudulent work. In effect the Statute meant that because English craftsmanship was bad, foreign cloths were sold at higher prices. Yet the prices were high mainly because foreign cloths were smuggled into England and the Statute was merely another attempt to protect bad workmanship and to stifle genuine, competitive trade.

So despite the fact that Edward IV was pro-Burgundian, the Duchy and England continued to legislate against one another. It was a ridiculous situation for natural allies. The Duke of Burgundy banned English cloths from coming into the Low Countries, and at the same time England prohibited the export of wares from the Low Countries into its own territory. Such regulations were almost self-defeating and they were circumscribed by new regulations aimed at curbing extravagance in dress. Thus, while nobles could wear whatever they pleased, no person under the rank of a lord could wear any purple silk; knights and their wives could wear no cloth of gold, or fur or sables; no esquires or gentlemen and their wives could wear any silk at all; no persons not having possessions of the annual value of £40 could wear any fur; no widow who had less than £40 in possessions could wear any fur, or any gold or silver girdle, or "any kerchief that had cost more than three shillings and fourpence".

In all these frustrating legislative forays William Caxton was closely involved. It is also evident that he, more than anyone else, realised the futility of these niggling prohibitions which allies placed upon each other and saw them not only as a stumbling block to a freer trade and prosperity but as positive obstacles to the alliance. By the time Edward IV came to the throne and Henry VI was imprisoned and deposed, Caxton had the ear of his King and of the Duke of Burgundy equally. In 1464 Edward IV issued a commission to "his trusty and well-beloved Richard Whitehill and William Caxton to be his especial ambassadors, procurators, nuncios and deputies to his most dear cousin, the Duke of Burgundy". Caxton was in effect given the task of either confirming an existing treaty of commerce, or, if necessary, negotiating a new one.[6]

The treaty was not reviewed during the reign of Philip the Good and in 1466 the Earl of Warwick ordered Caxton to enforce the penalties against the offenders. Caxton appealed to the Lord Mayor of London and the Mercers' Company against this retaliatory action, but they declined to take action either way. The accession of Charles the Bold changed all this. Two years later a treaty was concluded with the Duke of Burgundy by which trade between his domains and England, which had been interrupted for twenty years, was restored and a port of Flanders was subsequently appointed to be a port of the English staple as well as that of Calais. There is no question whatsoever but that this was a personal diplomatic triumph for Caxton.

4

At the Court of Burgundy

𝕴T had been as a result of pressure from the merchants of London, using the power and authority of their companies, that King Edward IV had been persuaded to allow Caxton a free hand in negotiations with the Duchy of Burgundy. In effect this made Caxton almost a personal envoy of the English King to the Duke of Burgundy, as the prestige of his royal master rested very much on what Caxton could achieve.

One must understand that Caxton had to contend with a xenophobic isolationism in England, more marked in the provinces and at the Court than in the City of London. He also needed to appreciate the Burgundian viewpoint which, while being much more flexible than that of the English, was nevertheless one of self interest. No one, however, was in a better position to assess the realities of the relative trading interest than Caxton himself.

Among his many duties as "Governor of the English Nation" in Bruges was that of seeing that all goods exported to England were of the correct weight and measure. Thus, any complaints concerning deficiencies in weight or measure detected in London were referred to him as is clear from a meeting of the Court of the Merchant Adventurers at Mercers' Hall on 16 August, 1465. William Redeknape, William Hande and John Sutton complained about the cloth they had received and it was recorded that a letter should be sent to "William Caxton, Governor beyond the Sea" asking him to set matters right, and to check this kind of abuse. The charter laying down the duties of the Governor of the English Nation had been implemented only two years before Caxton took office. They conferred full powers to govern and adjudicate, even extending to the Governor the authority to "make such minor regulations for the conduct of trade as might seem necessary, providing these did not cut across the obligations of international treaties". Armed with such authority, the Governor was much better able to negotiate with the Court of Burgundy. In addition he was authorised to settle all disputes between merchants and to pass sentences in a court comprised of himself and twelve justicers. There were many other duties of a minor, but still important nature, such as overseeing questions of weights and measures to supervising the sealing of parcels which left the city,[1] and all of which must have made his working day a long one.

Exacting as the duties of Governor of the English Nation were, they gave Caxton the status of a diplomat, and, in some respects, an adviser to the King. Another factor in his favour was that when, in 1467, Charles the Bold came to power at the Court of Burgundy, he married Margaret, the sister of Edward IV. It was with the Duchess Margaret that Caxton was soon to establish a long and fruitful relationship that greatly influenced his later career.

The whole story of relations between England and the Duchy of Burgundy over a long period had been one of intrigue and counter-intrigue. The Duke Philip had obtained lordship over the territories of Hainault, Holland, Zeeland and Friesland, but, declared Olivier de la Marche, Master of the Duke's household, "this succession, even though it was by hereditary right, he did not achieve without conquest. For the Lady Jacqueline of Bavaria, who succeeded to all the abovesaid countries, was a women of great ambition, and no less clever and subtle in making her will serve her desires.

"Although the good Duke Philip was her nearest relative, bad advice, wilfulness or whatever else made her forever seek and pursue dangerous alliances, contrary to the Duke's interest . . . intending to pass her territories to another hand, she went to England and sought to ally herself in marriage with the Duke of Gloucester . . . So the said Duke came to Hainault . . . and prepared an army under Lord Fitzwalter and sent it to Holland. To repel it, the Duke [of Burgundy] went in person, crossed the sea . . . and overcame the English . . . He agreed with the Lady Jacqueline that she remained nominal ruler of those said lands while he governed them for her."

This is an over-simplification of the real situation and somewhat glosses over the intrigues, but it is basically a true account of what happened. Philip built up his Duchy into a powerful realm in the heart of Northern Europe: in some respects it could be said to be a kind of medieval Benelux. When he died he was the richest prince of his time, leaving 400,000 gold crowns and 72,000 marks of silver plate quite

Charles the Bold, Duke of Burgundy, from a painting by Jean Van Eyck.
(*Radio Times*)

apart from a palace of treasures and a library of manuscripts that was envied far and wide.

Charles the Bold, Philip's successor, was impetuous where his father had been cautious. He was irked by the thought of being in any way dependent upon the support of the French King and almost immediately headed the league of vassal nobles against their suzerain, Louis XI of France, and with them fought the battles of Paris and Montlhéry

(1465). This was a venture which was rash rather than bold, for it resulted in a Pyrrhic victory which the French monarch was later to exploit. All this occurred before Philip's death. Once Charles was King he discarded the French alliance with the avowed aim of restoring the old Kingdom of Burgundy, to include Lorraine, Switzerland and the South of France. Philippe de Commines, a French chronicler of the time, wrote of Charles, Duke of Burgundy, that he "was governed by no counsel but his own: and whereas before he was altogether averse and unfit for war, and took delight in nothing that belonged to it, his thoughts were so strangely altered upon this that he spent the remainder of his life in wars, in which he died, and which were the occasion, if not quite of the ruin of his family, at least of the misery and desolation of it."[2]

This was the fire-eating, impulsive man with whom Caxton had to deal after the death of Philip. It should not be thought that because of Charles' antagonism to France that he was attracted to the English Court and Edward IV. The latter was a Yorkist, while the Duke of Burgundy's mother had belonged to the House of Lancaster. With the wounds of the Wars of the Roses far from being healed, the Court of Burgundy had received refugees of the Lancastrian cause and shown them pronounced favour. Commines wrote that some of these refugees from England "were reduced to such extremity of want and poverty before the Duke of Burgundy received them, that no common beggar could have been in greater need . . . I saw one of them, who was Duke of Exeter (but he concealed his name), following the Duke of Burgundy's train bare-foot, begging his bread from door to door; this person was the next of the House of Lancaster; had married King Edward's sister; and being afterwards known, had a small pension allowed him for his subsistence. There were also some of the Somersets and several others, all of them slain since, in the wars."[3]

But the Duke of Burgundy was not one to let sentimental ties stand in the way of his policy-making. Despite his close family associations with the House of Lancaster, he now turned his attention to the Yorkists and King Edward IV. So determined was he to discard the Lancastrians and to woo the Yorkists that, within a year of his accession to the throne, he married Margaret, sister of Edward IV. What part Caxton played in this marriage must be purely conjectural, for he tells us nothing on the subject. Commines said that the marriage was "principally to strengthen the alliance against the King of France, otherwise he would never have done it, for the love he bore the House of Lancaster".[4]

Preparations for the marriage in which, to some extent, Caxton would have been involved on account of his position as Governor of the English Nation, would have provided a welcome change in his life. For not only was his position a lonely one, but life in the confines of the English merchants' enclosure was restricted and dull. Foreigners were regarded by the natives of Bruges with some suspicion and much dislike and, for their own protection as much as a preference for herding together, the English merchants dwelt inside the barracks-like *Domus Anglorum*. There they worked, ate at a common table, and slept. It was much like living in a boarding school with a curfew each night when each member was supposed to be inside the enclosure. Marriage was impossible in such conditions and no woman was allowed on the premises.

Prior to the arrangement of this royal marriage Caxton had had an irksome time in Bruges, frequently being hampered in his relations with the Burgundians by blunders in policy-making and ignorant interference by some authorities in London. Most of his difficulties had been concerned with the renewing of the trade treaty which ended in November, 1465. When the question of renewing the treaty was first raised in October, 1464, a year before it was due to end, the English King had asked Sir Richard Whitehill, an able and experienced diplomat, and Caxton to confer with the Burgundians. This attempt was unsuccessful and afterwards the Mercers' Company requested Caxton to conduct talks with the Company's other members in Bruges on what the next step should be. One must bear in mind the normal procedure for promotion within the Mercers' Company. There does not seem to have been any definite period between taking the freedom of the City and making the Livery payments. One can only guess at Caxton's progress and such guesses are not made easier by the fact that, according to the Plea and Memoranda Rolls of the City of London, it would seem that the widow of a merchant was expected to maintain the husband's apprentices and ensure they learned their trade.

Johanna, who was a widow when she married Robert Large, had a considerable fortune of her own. When Robert died she appeared to be deeply distressed, solemnly proclaiming at his graveside that she would: "avow to God . . . to live in chastity and cleanness of my body from this time forward as long as my life lasteth, never to take other spouse but only Christ Jesu." The spirit was willing, but the flesh was weak: within three years she was married for a third time, on this occasion to John Gedney, a draper. Stow, in his *Survey of London* recorded that when they married: "they were troubled by the Church, and put to penance, both he and she."

The trading situation between England and Burgundy was exacerbated by the decision of the Duke of Burgundy to exclude all English-made cloth from his realm and this was countered by a move in London to ban the import of Flemish goods into England by Act of Parliament. The English and the Burgundian merchants were determined that their trade should not be ruined and they continued business by smuggling their goods to each other through neighbouring territories. Caxton was well aware of this and the situation was not helped when the Earl of Warwick wrote to him, demanding a rigid enforcement of the Act of Parliament forbidding the purchase of Burgundian goods by English traders. Caxton's response was to write to the Lord Mayor of London and the Mercers' Company inquiring their views on this matter. Their reply was unhelpful and gave Caxton little scope for showing any flexibility in his dealings with the Burgundians. He was told that the Act of Parliament must be upheld in every possible way and that fines must be enforced.

It was not until the Duke Charles raised the question of his marriage to the Princess Margaret of England that the situation changed overnight. From that moment Caxton was in high favour at the Court of Burgundy and England was once again a much desired ally. Lord Hastings and Lord Scales were sent as envoys to Bruges to thrash out the details and finalise the treaty of marriage. That Caxton's role in all this was much appreciated on both sides seems evident from the fact that Lord Scales, later the second Earl Rivers, eventually became Caxton's chief patron, and that Princess Margaret took a keen interest in him from then on.

The marriage was celebrated in Bruges on 5 June, 1468, amidst great display of pageantry and splendour. John Paston, one of the Princess's retinue, describing the wedding scene, said: "As for the Duke's Court, as for the lords, ladies and gentlemen, I heard never of none like it, save at King Arthur's Court."[5]

Every Christian country sent an ambassador to the wedding. France sent the Lord High Constable, the Count de St. Pôl, who upset everyone and angered the Duke by arriving in the most ostentatious style with a large retinue of armed men, with trumpets and banners and pages on foot and a naked sword carried in front of him, an emblem of feudal sovereignty, impudently reminding his host that Burgundy owed allegiance to France. The Duke refused absolutely to receive the Count who from that day became his greatest enemy.

Tragedy marred the wedding. Among the chamberlains of the Duke of Burgundy was an illegitimate son of the Lord of Condé, a strikingly handsome young man of an agreeable disposition. He had fought beside the Duke at the battle of Montlhéry and was one of his favourites. The Bastard of Condé, as he was popularly known, had been playing a game of tennis when there was a dispute as to whether he had broken the rules. To settle the matter it was agreed to consult a canon of the Church who had been watching the game. The canon unhesitatingly ruled against the Bastard, who suddenly and almost inexplicably lost his normally equable temper and forgot his usual good manners. He raged at the canon who beat a hasty but dignified retreat to his residence. The Bastard followed with drawn sword and was confronted by the canon's brother who barred the way and begged forgiveness for the unfortunate cleric. The Bastard's reply was to kill the man instantly with his sword.

In many Courts in this period a favourite, such as the Bastard undoubtedly was, would have escaped without punishment after a killing like this and his crime would have been overlooked. Even at the Court of Burgundy it was generally expected that, in view of the imminence of the royal wedding and the fact that the young man was a favourite of the Duke, he would be reprieved. While the Bastard was under arrest at the house of the gate-keeper of the City of Bruges, representations in his favour were being made to the Duke. But Charles the Bold ignored these pleas and, just as he was about to set out to meet the Princess Margaret at the nearby port of Ecluse, he ordered that the Bastard should be executed the following morning. Despite this, the execution was delayed for several hours by the presiding magistrate in the hope that the Duke might relent at the last moment. No reprieve was made, however, and the Bastard of Condé was beheaded and his body divided into four quarters. It was not a pleasant prelude to the bridal festivities.

Charles and Margaret were pledged to one another at Ecluse in a simple ceremony and then Margaret was brought in a gilded and handsomely decorated barge by canal to Damme, where the marriage was solemnised. Afterwards she was escorted to Bruges in a litter surrounded by sixty ladies of England and Burgundy, mounted on hackneys. John Paston, writing to his mother in England about the wedding, said: "there were never Englishmen had so good cheer out of England that ever I heard of . . . my Lady Margaret was married on Sunday last past at a town that is called The Dame, three miles out of Bruges at five o'clock in the morning. . . . Many pageants were played in her way in Bruges to her welcoming, the best that ever I saw."[6]

This was a sober description of events compared to one Latin chronicler who wrote that: "the sun never shone upon a more splendid ceremony since the creation of the world!"

Yet the wedding festivities must have ranked with some of the most magnificent pageantry and splendour of the whole of the Middle Ages. After the dinner given in Margaret's honour the Court went to the Lists where a "grand exercise in chivalry" was enacted, based on the legend of the Tree of Gold. This legend was a rather more ornate, or perhaps one might say a rococo version of "Jack and the Beanstalk". A poursuivant at arms, in the livery of the Tree of Gold, presented to the Duke a letter from the Princess of the Unknown Isle, in which she offered her grace and favours to the knight who would capture the giant she had committed to the care of a dwarf. In the Lists was set up the huge gilded tree, at the foot of which was a dwarf with a giant held in chains.

Knights arrived in the Lists to take up the challenge and each in turn addressed a neat little speech of welcome to the Duchess. It all ended with the Bastard of Burgundy, the Count de la Roche, hero of many jousts, breaking the greatest number of lances and winning the ring of gold. This pageant-cum-tournament was followed by another banquet at which minstrels sang songs in praise of the "beautiful shepherdess of England". Song, dance, jousts and pageantry continued for eight days. On the last day of festivities there rolled into the grand hall a cunningly constructed model whale, sixty feet long, with a body large enough for a man on horseback to have hidden in it. The eyes of the whale comprised two huge mirrors and when its mouth was opened out of it climbed "a group of syrens . . . and a dozen marine knights".

It must have been within a year after the royal wedding that Caxton came to be directly employed by Margaret, Duchess of Burgundy. Immediately after the wedding celebrations negotiations for new trade treaties were set in hand and in these Caxton must have played a prominent role. Edward IV sent a mission to Burgundy with a view to stepping up the wool trade and putting it on a sounder basis, and the Mercers' Company, acting after consultation with the King, named Caxton, William Redeknape and John Pickering as members of this mission. This was in September, 1468. Caxton, of course, was almost an automatic choice as Governor of the English Nation. He was by then by far the most influential Englishman in the Low Countries, with a wide knowledge of all the ramifications of English trade on the continent.

It is clear that Caxton travelled outside Bruges quite often during this period, and the records of Utrecht show that between 1464 and 1468 free visas were granted to Caxton and his servants for visiting that important trading centre. He himself mentioned various visits to Holland, including one to Antwerp. In *The Golden Legend*, under the heading "David", Caxton made a brief reference to this period:

"For as I once was beyond the sea riding in the company of a noble knight named Sir John Capons, and was also doctor in both laws and was born in Malyorke . . . and that time Counsellor unto the Duke of Burgundy, it happened we communed of the history of David, and this said noble man told me that he had read that David did this penance . . . thus this noble man told me, riding between the town of Ghent in Flanders and the town of Brussels in Brabant."

But in the last two years of his term of office as Governor of the English Nation Caxton seems to have been more occupied with private work of some kind than with that of his official position. This may have been due to his already being engaged in unofficial duties for the Duchess of Burgundy, or it could have been that, on his own account, he had become immersed in the quest for manuscripts and the translations of them into English. It is not without some significance that

MARGARET DUTCHESS of BURGUNDY
Sister of Edward 4th King of England
An ancient Picture, in the poßeßion of T.KERRICH M.A.
Principal Librarian to the University of Cambridge

Published Nov.r 1st 1804, by Wm Richardson York House No 31. Strand.

Margaret, Duchess of Burgundy, sister of Edward IV; a patroness of Caxton.
(*Mary Evans*)

Caxton declared that he started work as a translator "as a preventive against idleness".

On 12 May, 1469, the records mention a dispute between an English and a Genoese merchant, which was referred to the Governor of the English Nation, and one Thomas Perrot. Caxton, according to the documents, was engaged on business outside Bruges—there is no indication of what it was—and in his absence a full court of merchants was called to arbitrate. The following month Caxton was probably concerned with the trade negotiations which were then in full session, while in August it was recorded that he was among a number of people who received "four kans of wine" from the Town Council of Bruges. This may have been a gift intended to commemorate the end of his term of office as Governor of the English Nation. Strangely, considering records were so carefully kept in those days, there is no mention of the date on which he left his post.

Sometime after June, 1469, Caxton must have unostentatiously entered the service of Margaret, Duchess of Burgundy, almost certainly in the capacity of a secretary, librarian or translator, or probably a combination of all three. Perhaps in the beginning Caxton performed other and more formal services for the Duchess; undoubtedly he was a welcome link with England and in a position to obtain goods duty free for his patron. But it was from what Caxton himself tells us of his association with the Duchess, that we learn what brought them together: a love of literature and discussions on the problems of language. Margaret had been well educated and was not only a patron of the arts, but anxious to see some of the best works of Europe translated into English, her native language. Caxton may also have come to her notice by his ability to obtain rare manuscripts for her. The Mercers in their trade with the continent had often been devoted as much to learning as to making money. They were the principal agents by which valuable manuscripts came into England, especially from the Low Countries. John Bagford, writing about Caxton in 1714, stated that: "Kings, Queens and noblemen had their particular merchants who, when they were ready for their voyage into foreign parts, sent their servants to know what they wanted, and, among the rest of their choice, many times books were demanded."[7] Caxton has admitted that he built up his own library in this way, specifically mentioning "a special friend, William Pratt, a Mercer", as finding for him French manuscripts.

It was while he was wrestling with the problem of translating *Le Fevre Recueil* that Caxton first mentioned the Duchess of Burgundy. He started this work in 1469, but then laid it aside, not apparently being satisfied with the progress he had made. It was while he was working for Margaret of Burgundy that she persuaded him to resume this work. Describing his frustrating endeavours in this period, Caxton wrote:

"After that I had made and written five or six quires, I fell in despair of this work, and purposed no more to have continued therein, and the quires laid apart; and in the two years after laboured no more at this work, and was fully in will to have left it. Till on a time it fortuned that the right high, excellent and right virtuous princess, my right re-doubted lady, my Lady Margaret . . . sent for me to speak with her good grace of divers matters, among the which I let her highness have knowledge of the aforesaid beginning of this work; which anon com-manded me to show the said five or six quires to her said grace. And when she had seen them, anon she found default in mine English, which she commanded me to amend, and moreover commanded me straightly to continue and make an end of the residue not then trans-lated. Whose dreadful commandment I durst in no wise disobey, because I am a servant unto her said grace, and receive of her yearly fee, and other many good and great benefits, and also hope many more to receive of her highness."[8]

This does rather suggest that Caxton was still loth to take up this work again, but that he dared not risk incurring the Duchess's dis-pleasure. It is the clearest picture we have of Caxton's position with Margaret, though it does not spell out his duties. It also intimates that the Duchess was a skilled critic, as conscious of the need for improving the still crude English language as she was of the lucidity and em-bellishments of French and Latin prose. She was as eager to see that continental literature was translated into English as Caxton himself had always been. But Caxton, who was no courtier, but merely a simple merchant, was perhaps too self-critical of his efforts and suffered from an inferiority complex. If anyone cured him of this it was the Duchess, for he declared that he "forthwith went and laboured in the said translation after my simple and poor cunning, all so nigh as I can, following mine author, meekly beseeching the bounteous highness of my said lady that of her benevolence list to accept and take . . . this simple and rude work."

It is now apparent that Caxton had for some few years been toying with the idea of translating European literature into English. Four months before Margaret came to Bruges he had commented that he had "no great charge or occupation" and that he began the work of translalation "for to pass therewith the time". Once the Duchess set him seriously to work on translations as part of his duties there could have been little respite. Indeed, Caxton could not have enjoyed the lighter side of Court life much, or indulged in its entertainments and frolics. Instead he was immersed in some lonely turret room in one of the towers of the palace at Bruges, busily scratching away with his pen, pondering on the right choice of words and no doubt crossing out and re-writing on many occasions.

Mr. N. F. Blake in his own deep study of Caxton is not happy about the lack of evidence as to exactly what duties Caxton performed for the Duchess of Burgundy. "Why Caxton should have wanted the patronage of Margaret of Burgundy is easily explained", writes Mr. Blake. "Margaret was the sister of Edward IV of England and her marriage to Duke Charles of Burgundy was a political one to strengthen the Anglo-Burgundian alliance. Because of her position she became the focal point for promoting English interests in the Low Countries. . . . There were also many Englishmen at Margaret's Court, including many members of the aristocracy. By becoming one of Margaret's protégés Caxton could further his acquaintance with them."[9]

One attraction which the Palace at Bruges would have for Caxton would be that it enabled him to have access to the magnificent library which the former Duke Philip had built up. There was also the library of Louis of Bruges, Seigneur de la Gruthuyse, Cup-Bearer to the Duke of Burgundy and Commander-in-chief of the Burgundian Court's garrison. An extremely wealthy man, Louis of Bruges was a great friend to England (for which he was made Earl of Winchester) and a passionate bibliophil. Most probably Caxton had himself helped to build up this library by the buying and selling of manuscripts, just as he may even have presented items to the Duchess's own library with a view to winning her favour. Louis of Bruges employed some of the finest scribes and illuminators in Europe to make copies of books for his library and had them bound in sumptuous silks and velvets with precious stones and gold to form the clasps.

Louis' library was still being formed when Caxton was in Bruges and here unquestionably the Englishman discovered many of those works which later he translated. Among the works in Louis' library were a copy of *Le Recueil des Histoires de Troye*, *Le Roman du Lancelot* and *Les Livres des Quatre Dames*.

Caxton was merely one of a number of translators employed at the Court of Burgundy. The Duchess Margaret gave assignments to various writers and translators to make books for her, including David Aubert and her almoner, Nicholas Finet. The knowledge that he was in effect competing with scholars may have aggravated Caxton's inferiority complex.

Meanwhile the Duke of Burgundy was pressing ahead with his new English alliance, continuing to oppose the French in every possible way and holding audiences every Monday and Wednesday. His custom was to go to the audience hall when he had finished his dinner, taking his seat on a chair richly covered in cloth of gold on a dais. Below him was a small bench at which sat the two masters of requests and the audiencer who read out petitions to the Duke. Philippe de Commines gave this account of the audiences: "The hall is surrounded by a large railed enclosure, all shut off with benches and balustrades, covered in hangings bearing the Duke's coat-of-arms. On the right side stand the Duke's esquire servers and cup-bearers, and on the left the carvers and esquires of the stables; they stand upright by the balustrades. In front of the rails are benches all round the enclosure where the knights, chamberlains and any strangers present sit, and also the masters of the household. . . . At the entrance and at the doors are ushers-at-arms, and by the gangway two sergeants-at-arms, each bearing a mace with the prince's arms. . . . When all is set two doors are opened on two sides of the hall; by the one enter those who bring petitions and present them to the Duke, and by the other they go out. . . . The Duke disposes of the petitions at his pleasure, and he deals with them all before he leaves the palace."[10]

There was plenty of prosperity at the Court of Burgundy in this era and Commines pays tribute to the aura of glory which surrounded it: "The subjects of the House of Burgundy lived at that time in great plenty and prosperity, grew proud and wallowed in riches . . . their entertainments and banquets more profuse and splendid than in any other place I saw."[11]

It was a fairy-tale world at the Court of Burgundy where merchants competed with noblemen in displays of splendour and the canals of Bruges were filled with boats laden with treasures from distant lands. It was a world from which Caxton himself was increasingly withdrawn into his ivory tower, there by the influence of the Duchess and through his own native determination and self-discipline, to make his gradual, but ultimately all-important contribution to the English Renaissance.

5

Caxton the Romantic

IN considering Caxton's life and even more his purposes in his later career, it is important to realise that he was one of the early English romantics. It is this romanticism which dominated in both his love of and choices in literature and which impelled him with the urge to adapt, improve and embellish the English language. Thus an unskilled, conscientious, but undistinguished writer was, through his translations, to pave the way for Shakespeare, Marlowe and Edmund Spenser. The word "renaissance" is not usually applied to William Caxton, yet without him English literature might have stood still for another fifty years.

It is notable that Caxton had a philosophy of his own and in many respects it was a romantic philosophy. In all his translations, sometimes interpolated into the text, more often in the prologues and epilogues he wrote to them, he made a point of expressing his own views. While being diffident about the quality of his work and self-critical of his abilities, he was quite certain about the direction in which he wished to influence events. And in this instinctive feeling that on broad principles he was right in what he was trying to do, Caxton was actuated by his romantic conception of man's duty in the world and his proper attitude to his fellow citizens. When he wrote that one should "do after the good and leave the evil, and it shall bring you good fame and fortune", he may have been making a trite remark, but the gist of his advice was almost identical with the Code of Chivalry. The tenth point of the Code of Chivalry urged "the championship of the right and the good in every place and at all times."[1]

G. M. Trevelyan said of Caxton that he "was an early and noble example of a well-known modern type that has done so much for the world, the individualistic Englishman, following out his own 'hobbies' with business capacity and trained zeal . . . His industry was prodigious. . . . He had indeed a missionary zeal for the dissemination of

good and useful books among his countrymen 'in our English language.' His diligence and success as a translator did much to lay the
foundations of literary English and to prepare the way for the great
triumphs of the following century."[2]

That Caxton was well aware of the unsatisfactory state of the
English language has already been shown, but no doubt it was the
Duchess Margaret who, either directly or indirectly, showed him how
unpolished a vehicle it was. Hitherto Caxton had realised that English
had unhappily remained a hotchpotch of several dialects, often with
little in common, and that some of them, like that of the Weald of Kent,
were rude and rough and lacking in any pretension to culture. He
makes no mention of exactly what Margaret criticised in his translation, but, one must assume, knowing that the Burgundian Court was
heavily steeped in the embellished French of the Troubadours and the
French prose style, described by Caxton as "compendious", that it was
probable that the Duchess thought his use of words was clumsy and
unornamented.

Certainly Caxton was under no illusions about the difficulty of his
task. He spoke of the "fair language of French" and its prose being
"compendiously set and written", and he obviously deeply regretted
that he had learned French at second hand and not lived in France. He
was always anxious to keep as close as possible to the original meaning
in French, when translating, but found that to do this often resulted in
losing almost completely the fineness of expression of the French text.
He was for ever striving after changing what he called "the rude and
old Englyssh".

At the time of his first efforts at translating *Le Fevre Recueil* Caxton
had a limited vocabulary in English, but this was a disadvantage which
he rapidly surmounted mainly as a result of his being at the Burgundian
Court. Some critics of Caxton have suggested that he owed an enormous debt to John Lydgate and to so ornate a writer as Skelton, tutor
to the Prince of Wales. Yet the truth was that by remarkable self-
discipline and self-teaching Caxton improved both his vocabulary and
usage of English by working backwards, that is to say, he kept closely
and faithfully to the French and Latin original texts and allowed the
niceties of style to filter through into an English that was rather more
in a poetic than a prose vein. Often this was achieved by unashamedly
borrowing French, or even Latin words and moulding them into an

English prose framework, or adapting and anglicising them. Thus he would write "Cecy estre demandé, il fut commandé",[3] aiming at making the pure gold of some French or Latin phrase to shine through the English translation. Margaret may have pointed out such a method to him as being one way out of his difficulties.

Yet why is it that the often crude, unmusical and mundane prose of Caxton had such an impact? He was a teacher (of the courtly style) who was unable to put into practice what he was constantly reiterating. He had neither the talent for original rhetoric and gift for style, nor the time in which to weave exquisite translations, bearing in mind the enormous amount of work he undertook. How he came to influence a future generation of Englishmen as writers was in the manner he achieved a break-through in the language. It was as though he deciphered the English language, eliminating the arcane and obsolete dialect words, substituting French and Latin adaptations as he saw fit, almost like fitting out of a jig-saw puzzle and in some almost esoteric process bringing the languages of the continent and the King's English close together. This merging of cultures through translation did not make the English language of the Renaissance period, but it helped to speed up the process of acquiring a national language of imagery, embellishment and style.

N. F. Blake takes the view that Caxton probably exaggerated the difficulties of translation and that, when he wished, he could translate with a fair speed and fluency. It is true that modesty was held to be essential in any scribe in this period and it was the custom when "offering" a book to a patron to beg tolerance for the faults in the prose and show due humility. In the case of Caxton this humility was possibly all the more marked because he felt ashamed to admit that he came from the Weald of Kent, which had the reputation of being an area of little refinement in those days. To admit one came from the Weald where wild and rebellious men were always marching on London and stirring up trouble was probably the fifteenth century equivalent of confessing to having learnt the English language in the Gorbals.

Nevertheless in Caxton's case there seems to have been a wistful feeling that, had he been born elsewhere, he might himself have belonged to that band of knightly brothers for whom he had such an admiration. Though his career gave him no opportunity for deeds of arms and chivalry, he always cherished ideals of knighthood and regretted that he could not himself be one of the noble band. His dedication to romantic literature was a form of escape into this mystic realm, half fairy-tale and half reality. That Caxton persevered with translations until the end of his days rather than embarking on original prose of his own was merely a reflection of the times, but it also revealed Caxton's love of the romantic literature of the Age of Chivalry which was now drawing rapidly to an end in medieval Europe. He was a great lover of the deeds and stories of chivalry. Among the books translated by him were *The Order of Chivalry, or Knighthood, Feats of Arms of Chivalry, The History of Godfrey of Boulogne, or the Conquest of Jerusalem,* and perhaps the most important and influential of all his romantic works, *The Noble Histories of King Arthur and of Certain of His Knights.*

The Order of Chivalry was a French work describing the duties, rites and conditions of a knight's life, "which book", wrote Caxton, "is not requisite to every common man to have, but to noble gentlemen that by their virtue intend to come and enter into the noble order of chivalry, the which in these late days has been used according to this book heretofore written, for forgotten, and the exercises of chivalry not used, honoured nor exercised as it has been in ancient times, at which the noble acts of the knights of England that used chivalry were renowned through the universal world."

This is the essential voice of Caxton, for once going beyond the bounds of translation and making what is almost a heartfelt plea for the restoration of the ideals of Chivalry. After referring to "that noble King of Britain, King Arthur, with all the noble knights of the Round Table, whose noble acts and noble chivalry of his knights occupy so many large volumes", he goes on to say: "Oh, ye knights of England, where is the custom and usage of noble chivalry that was used in the [past]. What do ye now but go to the bagnios[4] and play at dice? . . . Leave this, leave it, and read the noble volumes of Saint Grail, of Lancelot, of Galahad, of Perceforest, of Parsival, or Gawain, and many more. There ye shall see manhood, courtesy, gentleness. And look in later days of the noble acts since the Conquest, as in King Richard's days, Coeur de Lion; Edward I and III and his noble sons . . . Alas, what do ye but sleep and take ease, and are all disordered from chivalry. I would demand a question, if I should not displease: how many knights be there now in England that have the use and exercise of a knight? That is to wit, that he knows his horse and his horse him; that is to say, he being ready at a point to have all things that belong to a knight, a horse that is according and broken after his hand, his armour and harness meet and fitting, and so forth, etc. I suppose [if] a due search should be made, there should be many found that lack. The more pity [it] is. I would it pleased our sovereign lord that twice or thrice a year, or at the least once, he would do cry jousts of peace,★ to the end that every knight should have a horse and harness, and also the use and craft of a knight, and also to tourney one against one, or two against two, and the best to have a prize, a diamond or jewel such as should please the prince. This should cause gentlemen to resort to the ancient customs of chivalry to great fame and renown. And also to be always ready to serve their prince when he shall call them or have need. Then let every man that is come of noble blood and intends to come to the noble order of chivalry read this little book and do there-after in keeping [with] the lore and commandments therein com-prised."

In the same vein Caxton wrote into his *History of Godfrey of Boulogne* that "the high courageous deeds and valiant acts of noble, illustrious and virtuous persons are worthy to be recounted, put in memory and written, to the end that there may be given to them a name immortal by sovereign praise." His lament for the lost culture of chivalry in England may to some extent have been conditioned by a knowledge of the brutalities of civil strife during the Wars of the Roses when many unknightly deeds were committed on both sides. But it was also influenced by what he had seen and heard at the Court of Burgundy. No doubt Caxton had been inspired by the creation in Burgundy of the Order of the Golden Fleece by Philip the Good.[5] He certainly visited the great chamber of the Castle of Hesdyn where Philip ordered the legend of the Golden Fleece to be vividly illustrated and where, as he has it, "a subtil engyn could reproduce thunder, lightning, rain and snow". But his imagination would have been stimulated by the feats of his patron, Anthony Woodville, second Earl Rivers, who was one of the most distinguished knights of the fifteenth century, not merely a soldier and jouster, but a translator and poet. Woodville was *par excellence* a superb example of that courtly tradition of Chivalry with a

★ Arrangements for a tournament.

Anthony Woodville, Earl Rivers, one of Caxton's patrons. (*Radio Times*)

capital "C", allied to a love of learning and the arts to which Caxton himself subscribed. Here was a knight who not only kept the rules of courtly conduct, but had a zest for adventure and travel and romantic pilgrimages. In the Middle Ages one of the places of pilgrimage favoured by archbishops, kings, knights and humble people alike was the shrine of Saint James of Compostella in Galicia. Woodville made this pilgrimage and *en route* was given a French manuscript of the sayings of ancient philosophers which he later translated.

Anthony Woodville's most famous feat of arms was his two-day tournament which he fought with Anthony of Burgundy at Smithfield in 1467. The story which led up to this epic encounter was one which would have enthralled the sentimental and romantic Caxton. On 15 April, 1465, after he had been to high mass, Anthony Woodville had a talk with his sister, Elizabeth, wife of Edward IV. Describing this incident, he commented: "I drew me to the Queen of England . . . And as I spake to her ladyship on knee, the bonnet from mine head, as me ought . . . the ladies of her company arrived about me; and they of their benevolence tied about my right thigh a collar of gold garnished with pearls . . . And to that Collar was tied a noble flower of souvenance, enamelled and in a manner of an emprise."

The "flower of souvenance" was a keepsake to be held as a reminder that it was intended to encourage some knightly feat. Sometimes it was a real flower plucked at random, sometimes an artificial one, made of jewels. Anthony found in his bonnet a small parchment, sealed and tied with a golden thread. The sequel to this incident was that he went to see the King to request permission for a knightly exploit which resulted in the Smithfield tournament of June, 1467. This was two years after the challenge was made, as the Knight of Burgundy was unable to travel earlier.

On the first day of the contest the two knights fought on horseback, first with lances, then with swords. Anthony of Burgundy was toppled from his horse in one encounter and he alleged that Woodville had used an illegal weapon to cause his fall. Woodville replied by riding up to the King to show his equipment and to prove he carried no such weapon. Presumably he was exonerated. On the second day the two knights fought with axes and the fiercest of all the contests was stopped by the King when he threw his staff into the lists as a signal that combat was to end.

The two knights left the lists with their axes in their hands to show that they had not been disarmed. But Woodville had nearly killed his opponent, which was one reason why the King stopped the contest, and the chronicler of the joust commented: "And soon were they departid, to the honour of Lord Scalys for both dayes."

The Code of Chivalry and all it implied were constant pre-occupations, if not obsessions, of Caxton. It is not merely, as some have suggested, that Caxton was paying polite lip service to the customs of the day. As we have seen, those customs were already decaying and Caxton fervently believed that "the knightly life" was the basis of national morality and an inspiration for all classes of the community. The talk at the Court of Burgundy, if not in the City of London, or the *Domus Anglorum* of Bruges, was always of tournaments and deeds of daring, of ladies issuing challenges and flowers of souvenance to their chosen heroes. Caxton would have heard of the encounter between his patron, Anthony Woodville, and the Burgundian knight, but he must also have actually witnessed Anthony breaking eleven lances in the tournament held during the nine-day celebrations in Bruges at the marriage of the Duke Charles and Margaret. On this same occasion Anthony's brother, Sir John Woodville, was awarded the tournament prize.

It has been said that Caxton was dazzled and bemused by all the colour, pageantry, ostentation, quixotry and romance of tournaments and knightly deeds. "He did not see the cruelty and pride, the oppression and injustice that lurked beneath the glittering armour and the velvet mantle," wrote Charles Knight.[6] This is not quite fair. Caxton would have been well aware of the abuses of the system of Chivalry and of occasions when the Code was broken, as in the case of the Bastard of Condé. His own plea for a stricter adherence to the Code of Chivalry is surely an indication of his consciousness of the repeated failures to live up to it. Clearly he believed that in England at least the Wars of the Roses had helped to destroy the ideals of knighthood and chivalry. Constantly before him must have been the sad fate that befell Sir John Woodville, and his father, the first Earl Rivers.

Richard Woodville, the father of Anthony and John, was a humble knight who secretly married Jacquetta, the widow of the Duke of Bedford, brother of Henry V. Though fined one thousand pounds for this breach of etiquette, the couple were pardoned by Henry VI. Later Richard was not only received back into favour, but made a Knight of the Garter and created Baron Rivers. His daughter, Elizabeth, married Edward IV and he became High Constable of England in 1467. Then, in 1469, Richard Woodville was taken prisoner at Edgecote and, with his son, John, summarily executed at Kenilworth without being given the benefit of a trial. Anthony Woodville suffered a similar fate, but this tragedy belongs to a later chapter.

Five years after he produced his *Book of the Order of Chivalry* Caxton, who had obviously been pondering the lessons of events in England and the decline of knightly chivalry, took his theme a stage further.

This time (1489) he translated *Feats of Arms and Chivalry* "to the end that every gentleman born to arms and all manner of men of war, captains, soldiers, victuallers and all other, should have knowledge how they ought to behave them in the faits of wars and of battles."

This was a translation of the work of a remarkable woman, Christine de Pisan, who had originally dedicated this treatise on feats of arms and conduct in the lists and in battle to Minerva, goddess of wisdom and war. Christine's works were immensely popular at the Court of Burgundy. She married at the age of fifteen and before she was twenty was left a widow with three children to support. Incredibly for her day and age she succeeded on her own account and even ventured into the realm of men in writing this warlike treatise with a keen insight into martial tactics and customs. It was Christine who also wrote *Les Dits Moraux des Philosophes* which was later translated by Earl Rivers and printed by Caxton under the title of *The Dictes and Sayings of the Philosophers*. This was the first of Caxton's books to supply the date on which it was printed—18 November, 1477.

Conservative through his training in the City of London, romantic by temperament and through being brought into contact with the world of chivalry at the Court of Burgundy, Caxton was also a devout Catholic. Perhaps because of this he tried very hard to equate chivalry with his religion which, indeed, he might well have done in all truth had the Code of Chivalry been observed as it was originally set out. When Léon Gautier, a French scholar who had spent many years studying the history of chivalry, worked out what he described as the Decalogue, or Ten Commandments of the Code of Chivalry, some eighty years earlier, it was apparent that Christianity was the basis of the knightly cult. "Willingness to defend the Church", "Unswerving belief in the Church", "merciless war against the infidel", "strict obedience to the feudal overlord", *but* only "as long as those duties did not conflict with duty to God".[7] The message was clear: military glory alone was not enough. The true knight was a Christian soldier who also conducted his whole life, private and public, on Christian lines.

But the Crusades, intended as they were to further the causes both of Christianity and chivalry and to bind knights to the service of Christianity, rapidly degenerated into piratical and brutal raids in quest of loot, carried out by the European Crusaders with a ferocity and barbarity that far exceeded anything the Saracens committed. It is certain that Caxton could never have realised how the name of Christianity and the cause of chivalry were besmirched by the Crusades for the history of these battles as told by Christian scribes was totally biased and dressed deeds of slaughter and destruction as though they were the romantic epics of knighthood. But Caxton did realise he was living in an age that was approaching great changes, that religion itself was undergoing some changes, with the ancient power of the Church being lost to that of the laity, and that the Christian element in the Code of Chivalry was being ignored. He may, too, have drawn certain conclusions from what he had heard of the Children's Crusades, the impelling idea of which was that children, who were innocent, would be able to accomplish what men, who were sinful, were unable, or not permitted by God, to achieve.

The Reverend John Lewis wrote that Caxton "expressed a great sense of religion and wrote like one who lived in the fear of God and was very desirous of promoting his honour and glory."[8] Then he went on to criticise Caxton for being "so far carried away by the established errors and superstitions of his time as to be an advocate for some of the worst of them: as engaging in what they then called the Holy War, or marching armed forces into the land of Judaea to recover that and the city of Jerusalem out of the hands of the Turks."[9] This is somewhat unfair to Caxton: with nothing but prejudiced history available to him, he could be forgiven for not being more discerning. Lewis seems to be referring to the prologue to Caxton's translation of *The Siege and Conquest of Jerusalem by Christian Men, or Godfrey of Bologne*, when Caxton wrote that "Then I thus visiting this noble history, which is no fable nor feigned thing, but all that is therein true; considering also the great puissance of the Turk, great enemy of our Christian faith, destroyer of Christian blood, an usurper of certain empires and many Christian royaumes and countries." Yet if the reverend gentleman had read further on, he should have noted that Caxton went on to make a very strong plea for Christian unity and peace in a comment which shows him not merely to have been a good Christian, but a good European. For Caxton declared that it seemed to him "necessary and expedient for all Christian princes to make peace, amity and alliance each with other, and provide, by their wisdoms, the resistance against him, for the defence of our faith and mother, Holy Church, and also for the recuperation of the Holy Land and Holy City of Jerusalem, in which our Blessed Saviour Jesus Christ redeemed us with his precious blood . . . Thus, for the exhortation of all Christian princes, lords, barons, knights, gentlemen, merchants and all the common people of this noble royaume, Wales and Ireland, I have emprised to translate this book of the Conquest of Jerusalem, out of French into our maternal tongue . . . to encourage them [for] . . . recuperation of the said Holy Land."

Caxton believed that there should be something like a renewed Crusade to bring the Middle East under Christian rule and to achieve this he was anxious to see Christian Europe wholly united. Godfrey of Boulogne, or of Bouillon, was his ideal knight and probably one of the chief influences on Caxton's romantic philosophy.

Nominated as the first King of Jerusalem, Godfrey had refused to accept the title because he did not wish to wear the crown of a king in the city where Jesus Christ had worn a crown of thorns. In the Latin sacristy of the Church of the Holy Sepulchre in Jerusalem, Godfrey's sword and spurs are still preserved, a reminder of the esteem in which this knight was held by the Church, and confirmation of the description of him by William of Malmesbury as "that brilliant mirror of Christian nobility in which, as a splendid ceiling, the lustre of every virtue was reflected".

As Caxton re-discovered these legends of chivalry so he became determined to perpetuate them through translations. It is not putting too fine a point on his intentions to say that love of chivalric legends was a constant spur to his always laboured efforts at translation and that, later in life, it was one of the driving factors in his urge to print books in the English language. Increasingly, as he grew older, Caxton delved into the distant past for other legends in the tradition of chivalry, not only on the continent, but in England and even in Wales. He was fascinated by the legends of King Arthur and the Knights of the Round Table, which, contrary to general opinion, he seems first to have heard of from reading the works of Nennius, the Welsh historian who lived around A.D. 800, and not from the French texts which he only came across later. In some respects *The Noble Histories of King Arthur and Certain of His Knights*, in a folio of 432 leaves, represented the pinnacle of his printing achievements. Once again he made an exhortation in his prologue, urging "noble lords and ladies to read this said book". Within its pages, he added, almost in the vein of

Chaucer, would be found "many joyous and pleasant histories, and noble and renowned acts of humanity, gentleness and chivalries". It was at the end of the prologue that he made his punch line: "herein may be seen noble chivalry, courtesy, humanity, friendliness, hardiness, love, friendship, cowardice, murder, hate, virtue and sin. Do after the good and leave the evil, and it shall bring you good fame and fortune."

The legends of King Arthur had, of course, percolated to the continent and Caxton would probably have heard various French versions at the Court of Burgundy. He had originally had doubts as to whether the legends were anything but fables, possibly because Nennius lived two centuries after Arthur was supposed to have existed, while an earlier historian, Gildas, who would have been a contemporary of Arthur, made no mention of the King whatsoever. Obviously Caxton, despite all the snide criticisms that he was a semi-educated entrepreneur, often totally out of his depth in literary matters, had studied the Arthurian controversy in great detail. In his prologue to *King Arthur* he wrote that there were "many noble volumes be made of him and of his noble knights in French which I have seen and read beyond the sea". Yet, having originally had doubts as to the authenticity of the Arthurian legends, Caxton made it clear in his prologue that he was eventually convinced that Arthur was a real person. He admitted, in reply to those noblemen who had inquired why earlier on he had not printed a book about King Arthur, that many regarded Arthur as a fiction (a belief he had at one time shared), but that "one in special said that there were many proofs of his existence".

Caxton did not in this instance indicate who specifically asked for this work to be produced. Though most critics suggest that somebody coaxed Caxton into translating and printing this work, it is possible that he wished above all else to do this of his own accord. This may have been done in co-operation with someone else, for, as Caxton himself declared, the book was written after "a copy unto me delivered". Here it seems that he was hiding the identity of his patron, if indeed he had a patron in this instance.

Help on such a project he probably had, but it is more likely that this was one book which Caxton was determined to tackle regardless of whether or not he had a patron. Contemporary evidence is that Caxton was sufficiently a romantic to wish to translate and print the Arthurian legends regardless of whether he had a patron or not. This is not to deny that in many respects Caxton was probably a snob, that he translated and printed those items which the Courts of England and Burgundy desired, whether or not he preferred to tackle other works. In such an age Caxton could hardly have avoided publishing in the main what the respective Courts wanted. Critics writing in the twentieth century seem to show a total refusal to acknowledge that in the fifteenth century things were different: that there was no underground press, no popular press and that to make people aware of the benefits of the newly discovered arts of printing it was essential to reproduce what was popular in the one circle able to encourage and subsidise the new art—the Court.

It would seem, however, that occasionally Caxton pursued his own inclinations even against the trend of general opinion. He may have had discreet, but silent admirers such as the Woodvilles. But his belief in the Arthurian legends after having been sceptical of them was such that he may well have decided to go ahead without a patron, or for purposes of self respect, hinting at an anonymous one. The basis for Caxton's own change of opinion would seem to lie in a manuscript of a Warwickshire knight, Sir Thomas Malory, from which he worked.

As the testimony of Malory is still, even today, the subject of considerable dispute and argument, an examination of Caxton's sources on King Arthur is almost essential in assessing his judgement in such matters. One must always remember that Caxton was not a scholar, but merely a persevering, self-educated merchant who took a delight in learning. Malory obviously convinced Caxton that he had some substantial reasons for accepting the Arthurian legend, yet curiously Caxton was sufficiently critical of Malory's use of the English language that he treated it and re-wrote it with considerably less respect than more recent translators. It would seem that Caxton relied on Malory for the facts, but borrowed extensively from the more polished French records of the legends for the style. At any rate Caxton was a remarkably strict sub-editor of Malory, pruning, condensing and colouring as he saw fit.

There are still some critics who insist that there is no real proof of the existence of the Malory manuscript. William Blades does not help at all in this respect, for the truth is that diligent as Blades was as a biographer, he never quite assimilated the all important factual background to Caxton's life and times. All Caxton himself has to say about

Malory is that the knight finished his work "in the ninth year of the reign of King Edward IV", which would be in 1470, and that Sir Thomas had "reduced" his manuscript "from certain books in French". These French works, which concern the romances of Lancelot, Merlin, Tristram, the quest for the Holy Grail, and Arthur himself, are in manuscript form in the British Museum.

Malory is not, however, such an obscure figure as has generally been made out. He had been a Member of Parliament and had served in the French wars with Richard de Beauchamp, Earl of Warwick, but he was not exactly the ideal figure of English knighthood, which Caxton, as a contemporary, should have known. A search of the Public Record Office shows that he had been guilty of a long list of crimes both against the civil law and society and against the Code of Chivalry. The man who had worked so lovingly on the stories of Arthur and the Knights of the Round Table had sufficiently forgotten his knightly duties as to be a thief, a cattle rustler and an almost incurable criminal. He had used battering-rams to break down the doors of the Abbey of the Blessed Mary at Coombe, stealing jewels and ornaments. A good many years of his life were spent in prison and it was while he was serving a sentence that he wrote up the Arthurian stories.

In recent times there have been various claims that Malory manuscripts have been found and authenticated. The knight was first identified by Professor Kittridge in his work, *Who Was Sir Thomas Malory?* (1895) as Sir Thomas Malory of Newbold Revell in Warwickshire, who appeared to have succeeded to the family estates about 1433. He died in 1471, according to the latest evidence. Thus, on Caxton's testimony, he only finished his work on the Arthurian legends a year before he died. This may have accounted for the ruthlessly condensed versions of the legends which, possibly in his haste to get the task finished, he compiled as though he was racing against the clock. What Malory achieved was in effect a drastic piece of sub-editing rather than a meticulous translation, if one can accept the alleged versions of his manuscript in which he is said to refer to himself as "a knight prisoner", while he also begged his readers "to pray that God sende hym good delyveraunce sone and hastely".

The puzzle remains to this day. How did Caxton come to acquire the manuscript of a knight languishing in prison? Did Malory bequeath his work to Caxton? Did Caxton amend, adapt, alter or add to Malory's text? N. F. Blake writes that Caxton did not alter the translations of Rivers, Worcester or Chaucer because he had "too much respect for the translators". But, he adds: "there are, however, two works which Caxton did alter considerably, Malory's *Morte Darthur* and Trevisa's translation of Higden."[10]

If one accepts Mr. Blake's thesis, then one must also cast aside doubts as to whether any authentic texts of Malory exist and turn to the evidence of Eugene Vinaver, professor of French language and literature at Manchester University. From Vinaver's edition of Malory it is clear that Caxton altered book five of Malory quite considerably. Where Malory frequently used archaic English words and phrases, Caxton turned them into anglicised adaptations of French words. Above all Caxton took the crudities out of Malory's language, he embellished the prose slightly and put some of the conversational parts in more courtly phraseology. Mr. Blake sums it up by saying that: "Caxton attempted to print works written in what he considered to be the courtly style and when a book was not written in that style, he altered it to make it conform. . . . To Caxton and the fifteenth century it must have seemed as though Malory was the culmination of the old alliterative style rather than the beginning of another."[11]

Perhaps here lies a clue as to why nothing was done to ensure beyond all doubt the preservation of Malory's texts exactly as they were written. Professor Vinaver, an acknowledged expert on Malory, recently gave his opinion on the significance of the discovery of an early fifteenth-century chronicle of King Arthur and his knights in the library of Alnwick Castle, Northumberland. "The real significance of this find," he suggests, "could be that in the Middle Ages the distinction between fact and fiction was very slight indeed. Until now scholars and historians have made artificial distinctions between 'chronicles' and 'romances'." One can fairly safely assume that Arthur was not a King, but a sixth century military leader, fighting for the Britons against the Saxons, and later lovingly built up into a literary figure as glamorous as Charlemagne on that consistent medieval British principle that whatever the French can do, we can do better. The Arthurian legends are based on three certain sources—the continental versions such as those of the French, on which Malory himself drew; the Flemings who brought the stories from Wales, where they had been mercenary soldiers, to Holland at the end of the twelfth century; the

Welsh sources of Taliesin and Geoffrey of Monmouth; and, finally, such manuscripts as that discovered at Alnwick Castle.

One suspects that Caxton never met Sir Thomas Malory and knew very little about him. But somehow the knight's manuscript must have found its way into his hands sometime between Malory's death in 1471 and the printing of the work by Caxton in 1485. One problem for researchers in this field has always been that for many years the Caxton edition of *King Arthur* was the only one available for scholars to study. Not until 1934 did the discovery of a Malory manuscript lead to furious discussions on the authenticity of *Morte d'Arthur*, and indeed on just how many manuscripts on this theme Malory wrote. There are two possibilities as to why Caxton should have decided to translate the somewhat crude and old-fashioned English of a Warwickshire knight in preference to seeking out the French originals. One is that Caxton may already have stimulated such a desire among his clientele for romantic literature that he was pestered to produce similar books and the Arthurian legends would, of course, have made a natural choice. The other is that Caxton may have been toying with the idea of translating various versions of the Arthurian legends for a number of years, but had procrastinated because of the magnitude of the task. Then at last somebody presented him with a simple solution: the text of Malory's *Morte d'Arthur* was a drastic, but effective condensation of the stories of the legends. In effect Caxton had as a model a ready-made, rudely fashioned, but admirably, if ruthlessly abbreviated version: all he had to do was to remould the prose and make it more acceptable to nobles, if not to scholars. One must remember that, with but a few exceptions, Caxton was always writing for the nobility, or those in and around the Court.

It is even possible that Caxton was an unwilling translator of the Malory manuscript, possibly the only occasion on which he demurred at printing romantic literature. He may well have been pressed to accept the Malory text from a client and more or less ordered to print it. For years, even while he was fascinated by the Arthurian legends and trying to discover more about their origins, Caxton had been fully aware that many scholars refused to believe that Arthur had ever existed. This much he made clear in the reasons he gave for printing the book. At the same time he put on record that he was convinced of the existence of Arthur. This may have been a diplomatic conversion to such a belief, for it is hard to accept that he could have printed the book for nobles at the Court and at the same time expressed his doubts about its authenticity. Perhaps he salved his conscience by recording that there were dissentient views. He could not possibly claim that an English translation by a rascally knight in jail of French manuscripts could remove all doubt as to Arthur's existence.

Caxton certainly tidied up Malory's work and presented the material in such a way that King Arthur was the central figure in the whole series of episodes: "each small episode," writes N. F. Blake, "tends to become the illustration of a moral and can be read independently. The work has become something of a sermon on chivalry."[12]

It has already been noted that Caxton dealt most tersely with the Battle of Towton Heath. In editing the Arthurian legends he revealed a curious lack of interest in battles as such. Jousts, tournaments, feats of arms: all these things were lovingly dwelt upon, but he drastically cut out the details of battles. Caxton was much more interested in creating a picture of Arthur as a gallant, chivalrous Christian King who showed mercy to his enemies, helped the poor and protected woman and children.

Yet in his romanticism Caxton was not without a certain dry, whimsical humour. In printing Lord Rivers' translation of the French work, *Les Dicts Moraux des Philosophes,* he discussed the revision of this book with his patron and in an appendix he adds a chapter "touching upon women".

"I find that my said lord hath left out certain and divers conclusions touching women. Whereof I marvelled that my said lord hath not writ on them, nor what hath moved him so to do, nor what cause he had at that time. But I suppose that some fair lady hath desired him to leave it out of his book; or else he was amorous on some noble lady, for whose love he would not set it in his book; or else for the very affection, love and goodwill that he hath unto all ladies and gentlewomen, he thought that Socrates spared the sooth, and wrote of women more than truth; which I cannot think that so true a man and so noble a philosopher as Socrates was, should write otherwise than the truth. For if he had made fault in writing of women, he ought not to be believed in his other Dictes and Sayings. But I perceive that my said lord knoweth verily that such defaults be not had nor found in the women born and dwelling in these parts of the world. Socrates was a Greek born in a far country from hence, which country is all of other conditions than this is, and men and women of other nature than they be here in this country; for I wot tell of whatsoever condition women be in Greece, the women of this country be right good wise, pleasant, humble, discreet, sober, chaste, obedient to their husbands, true, secret, steadfast, ever busy, and never idle, attemperate in speaking and virtuous in all their works, or at least should be so. For which causes so evident, my said lord, as I suppose, thought it was not of necessity to set on his book the sayings of his author Socrates touching women. But forasmuch as I had commandment of my said lord to correct and amend where as I should find fault, and other find I none save that he hath left out these Dictes and Sayings of the Women of Greece, therefore in accomplishing his commandments, forasmuch as I am not certain whether it was in my lord's copy or not, or else peradventure that the wind had blown over the leaf at the time of the translation of his book, I purpose to write these same sayings of that Greek Socrates, which wrote of those women of Greece, and nothing of them of this royaume, whom I suppose he never knew."

This is the only instance of Caxton indulging in badinage with one of his patrons in what was a publically addressed work. Normally Caxton was deferential to the point of obsequiousness with his patrons. Here he not only queried why Lord Rivers had omitted the reference to women, but quite blatantly pulled his leg about it. One must assume the two men were in close accord and shared the same sense of humour.

Caxton's references to and views upon women were relatively few and always oblique: they appear to suggest a desire to look upon the fair sex in a romantic vein and to imbue them with all the virtues, while at the same time recognising that perfection in the female species is somewhat rare. "The women of this country be right good . . ." he says, and then as a snide aside adds "or at least should be so."

One book which he translated from the French and had printed in 1484 concerns the manners of women of the period. This is *The Knight of the Tower*, and in his preface to it Caxton makes it quite clear that he feels a Frenchman's view of feminine manners applies equally to the women of England. He states that the translating and printing of this book was at the request of "a noble lady which hath brought forth many noble and fair daughters, which be virtuously nourished". It is almost certain that this "noble lady" was Edward IV's Queen, Elizabeth

Woodville, and that the proposal for bringing out the book was made some three years earlier. But as in 1484 the Queen had sought sanctuary in Westminster Abbey along with the little Richard, Duke of York, her daughters, her son, Dorset, and her brother Lionel, Bishop of Salisbury, it is almost certain that at that time she was in no position to pay for this work, and the probability is that Caxton made a chivalrous gesture and published it at his own expense.

This would have been typical of the man. As for his translation of the book on feminine manners and customs, though it often seemed that Caxton was trying to make it seem a contemporary summary, Geoffrey of Latour-Landry, the original author, wrote his book in 1371. It was intended for the edification of his daughters. Curiously the work has been denounced by some as obscene and a corrupting influence, while others, Caxton among them, regarded it as essentially a moral work. In the light of modern controversy of what is and what is not obscene and corrupting, this particular book is of special interest. Caxton makes it abundantly clear that it is a work which: "I advise every gentleman or woman having children, desiring them to be virtuously brought forth, to get and have this book."

Nonetheless the book reveals some of those eternal frivolities of women: the Knight of the Tower complains of the levity of the ladies. "The wives say to their husbands every day, 'Sir, such a wife and such hath such goodly array that beseemeth her well, and I pray you I may have of the same.' And if her husband say to her, 'Wife, if such have such array, such that are wiser than they have it not,' she will say, 'No force it is [that is of no consequence], for they cannot wear it, and if I have it, ye shall see how well it will become me, for I can wear it.' And this with her words her husband must needs ordain her that which she desireth, or he shall never have peace with her, for they will find so many reasons that they will not be warned."

From this work it is clear that it was the habit of ladies to go freely to feasts, tournaments and feats of arms without their being accompanied by a husband or male relation. A contemporary writer says they corrupted their virtue by these freedoms. The "Knight of the Tower" warns women that if they abuse such freedoms or show indiscipline, they will be subject to harsh physical blows from their husbands. Yet the virtue of the women of the age was also typified in somewhat romantic manner. Of the Lady Cecile of Ballville the Knight of the

Tower says that "her daily ordinance was that she rose early enough, had ever friars and two or three chaplains, which said matins before her within the oratory. And after she heard a high mass and two low, and said her service full devoutly. And after this, she went and arrayed herself, and walked in her garden or else about her place, saying her other devotions and prayers. And as time was she went to dinner. And after dinner, if she wist, and knew any sick folk or women in their child-bed, she went to see and visited them, and made to be brought to them her best meat. And there as she might not go herself, she had a servant proper therefore, which rode upon a little horse, and bare with him great plenty of good meat and drink, for to give to the poor and sick folk such as they were. Also, she was of such custom that, if she knew any poor gentlewoman that should be wedded, she arrayed her with her jewels. Also she went to the obsequies of poor gentlewomen and gave there torches, and such other luminary as it needed thereto. And after she had heard evensong she went to her supper if she fasted not, and timely she went to bed, and made her steward to come to her to wit what meat should be had the next day."

6

The Mystery of Caxton's Marriage

ONE reason for so many of the mysteries, large and small, of Caxton's life story is that he was inhibited from putting on record too much about himself, partly because of a natural humility, which he frequently displayed and which was natural for the times in which he lived, but also because, as he was addressing his books to kings, duchesses, barons, knights and ladies of the Court, he felt it unseemly for a former merchant's apprentice to mention his own career.

As we have seen, his references to his birthplace, his parents and his education are so terse as to be almost uninformative. But Caxton was equally silent on a much more important matter—that of his marriage.

The earliest biographers of Caxton, in fact, assumed that he lived a celibate life and died a bachelor. Curiously, they seemed to take this for granted without attempting to make further inquiries. Caxton had never made any mention of a wife, he had given the impression of being disinterested in and critical of the usual human failings in matters of the flesh and there was the fact that in his earlier days, when for so many years he lived in Bruges in the English compound, he would neither have had the chance of marrying or of possessing a concubine. By the nature of his work in those days and even more by the monastic-like rigidity of the rules of the English compound, he would have been forced into celibacy.

Caxton was also somewhat of a puritan and often gave this impression in certain comments in the prefaces to his translations. It is true that there was probably a certain amount of hypocrisy about all this and that he was often trying to appear more respectable or upright than he was. But no breath of scandal seems ever to have disturbed his progress and in his lament of the degeneracy of fifteenth century life and the decay of the spirit of chivalry he had complained that knights did nothing "but go to the bagnios and play dice".

No record of Caxton having married has ever appeared. Nor, for that matter, has his will ever turned up, though it is clear that he must have made one judging by a law-suit after his death. As William Blades rightly says: "the discovery of Caxton's will would probably settle satisfactorily many questions about his family and relations, but all the registries in which it might possibly have been deposited have been searched without success."[1]

Yet Blades, with very little evidence to go on, was convinced that Caxton had married. At first it was little more than a hunch, unsupported by all his copious searches. Then, by a stroke of fortune in 1874, he was provided with a clue. A Mr. Gairdner, of the Public Record Office in London, discovered in the archives a document without any seals or signatures and which was therefore obviously a copy of the original, dated 20 May, 1496. This revealed that a dispute had arisen between one Gerard Croppe, a merchant tailor, of Westminster, and his wife, Elizabeth, "daughter of William Caxton", and that the case was brought before the Archdeacon and the King's Chaplain, who heard it in St. Stephen's Chapel, Westminster.

That this was beyond all reasonable doubt the daughter of Caxton the printer was made clear from the proceedings of the case. The court decided that the couple should live apart and that neither should "vex, due or trouble" the other for any manner or cause, each being bound over in the sum of £100 to keep this promise. Then came the part of the judgement which clinched the issue of the relationship. This stated:

". . . And thereupon the said Gerard to have of the bequest of William Caxton, the fadre of the said Elizabeth, XX[ti.] prynted legendes at Xiijs iiij d a legend. And the said Gerard to delyver a general acquittaunce unto the executors of William Caxton her said Fadre, for their discharge in that behalf."[2]

Doubtless the bulk of Caxton's estate comprised the remainder of the books he had printed and which remained in stock. In this period—and indeed for the next hundred years or more—it was learning and scholarship, the purchase of books and the building up of libraries which impoverished men rather than riotous living, or more frivolous activities. In the reign of the first Elizabeth, John Dee, another inquisitive scholar, complained of the cost of books and how he had to sell family treasures to purchase more. Throughout his life he paid heavily and frequently ran into financial problems through collecting books. It would not be quite the same in Caxton's time, but he could not always have relied on visiting libraries at no cost at all. It is certain that he had to spend money in obtaining manuscripts and in finding rare works to translate. Whatever he may have earned was almost certainly ploughed back into the cause of printing, despite the help he received from his patrons. Indeed, in all probability it was not merely the rigid rules about celibacy maintained in the English compound at Bruges which held him back from marriage for some years, but his single-minded devotion to the translating of books. Though his will is missing, it is certain that he made one as in the parish accounts of St. Margaret's, Westminster, for the years 1496–1498 among the legacies listed as "bequothen to the Churche behove by William Caxton" are various printed books, entitled *Legendes*. These are undoubtedly the "prynted legendes" referred to in the law-suit. In the year 1484 Caxton printed the first edition of his work, *The Golden Legend*, based on the work, *Legenda Aurea*, by Jacobus de Voragine, Archbishop of Genoa, describing the lives and miracles of various saints. It was a translation from Latin, amplified by adaptations from the French and English, and in 1487 Caxton brought out a second edition of this book.

Thus Caxton unquestionably had a daughter and all the indications of the court case between her and her husband indicate that she was legitimate. So he must have had a wife. But who was she? In 1490 the death and burial at St. Margaret's, Westminster, of one "Mawde Caxton" is duly recorded. Among the burial fees mentioned in the accounts the following item appears: "Item atte Bureyng of Mawde Caxston for torches and tapres iijs ljd".

There is, however, no further clue as to whose wife "Mawde Caxston" was, and, as we have noted, though William Caxton lived in this parish in this period, there were other Caxtons, Caxstons and Caustons. Yet the probability is that she was William's wife and that she died not long before her husband.

As to when and where he married, this is a matter of pure speculation. William Blades gives his opinion, with which few subsequent biographers have quarrelled, that Caxton "could not have married much later than 1469". Blades based this deduction on the fact that if Caxton had married in that year and his daughter had been born within a year, she would have been twenty-one at the time of her father's death and twenty-six when the case against her husband was heard.

Certainly the regulations of the English community in Bruges would have debarred Caxton from anything other than a secret marriage before he left his post as Governor of the English Nation and entered the service of the Duchess Margaret of Burgundy. It would seem therefore from this that any recognised marriage would have been solemnised at some time between 1469 and 1475, but a secret marriage cannot altogether be ruled out. The very fact that there is no record whatsoever of a marriage either in Bruges, or elsewhere on the continent, or in England, might seem to point to Caxton having been married secretly possibly during the period that he was Governor of the English Nation. Where Blades made an error was in assuming that when Caxton stated that he had been thirty years overseas, he meant he had been away from England without a break all this time. We know that Caxton returned to London once on Mercers' Company business; it is probable that he made several such visits, perhaps even once a year, and that on one of these he could have been married. On the other hand it is perhaps more likely that he could have secretly married a woman in Bruges or elsewhere. It might even be that he had long wished to marry such a woman, but, being debarred by reason of the rules of the English community, entered the Duchess Margaret's service in order to be free to marry. Alternatively he may have married after he entered Margaret's service, possibly to someone employed at the Court.

If the "Mawde Caxton" mentioned in the parish records of St. Margaret's, Westminster was William's wife, then it would seem that she was probably English: that much is suggested by the name Mawde. Perhaps the likeliest answer to this mystery is that Caxton, who by the time he entered Margaret's service would have been either in his mid-forties or late forties, suddenly became determined to assuage his loneliness by marrying some simple, low-ranking Englishwoman who held a minor post in the Duchess's entourage. This could explain Caxton's somewhat hasty departure from Bruges and the hushing up of the wedding.

What emerges out of all of Caxton's work—and here the emphasis is on his translations rather than his printing—is that he must have been a very lonely man, detached and somewhat sad, much more removed from the world he lived in than many of the worldly, sophisticated priests of the period. One must always remember that it is

Caxton the translator who is important. Without being a translator it is extremely doubtful if he would ever have become a printer. He was in fact a deliberate celibate as dedicated to the cause of the written word as any ardent monk of the Dark Ages trying to preserve what was left of civilisation in the seclusion of his cell.

The longer Caxton lived the more he withdrew into himself, into the world of literature in which he could recreate his ideals and fantasies. He was not a scholar to whom learning came effortlessly. He was not a sophisticated all-rounder like Anthony Woodville, his patron, one who could mix learning and deeds of daring, quests for knowledge and jousting in the Lists. To Caxton the pursuit of knowledge must at times have seemed like a penance. Anyone who knows how frustrating and full of anguish detailed research into minutiae can be, even in the twentieth century with all its aids to such work, involving a temporary retreat from the world, should be able to understand that for Caxton it must have been a supreme effort in self-discipline, a constant fight against enormous odds—the limitations of the English language, the difficulties of translation, the fact that he had never visited France or Italy, those homes of the culture of the Middle Ages, the desire to be honest, yet the wish to please his readers, and, above all, the nagging feeling that he was neither a good translator nor a good linguist and that only relentless determination would enable him to succeed. One imagines he must have often worked far on into the night, bent over his manuscripts.

He would have had little opportunity for meeting women outside the precincts of the Court of Burgundy. It might even have been that the Duchess Margaret, taking compassion on him, found for Caxton the faithful mate who would run his household and leave him to his almost monastic devices. All this is guesswork and it cannot be otherwise. It is worth noting, however, that in the period 1469–72 Caxton faced one of the crises of his life. This was determined more by international politics than by any more mundane considerations.

In February, 1470, ambassadors were sent to Ghent by Edward IV to invest the Duke of Burgundy with the Order of the Garter. It was about this time that Caxton journeyed out of Bruges on numerous occasions—to Ghent, Antwerp and other places. Then in October, 1470, Edward IV, accompanied by some of his Court, went to Bruges to seek exile and escape from the plotting of the Earl of Warwick.

Edward IV, from an engraving of a painting in the possession of the Society of Antiquaries. (*Radio Times*)

Caxton was undoubtedly at hand during Edward's period of exile and would have acted as an intermediary for the royal party with the Court of Burgundy, for the royal patronage accorded him dates from about this time.

Edward IV was the antithesis of Henry VI. Whereas the latter, an unworldly ruler whose compassion was mistaken for weakness, had sought refuge among his clergy away from the trials of kingship,

Edward was an extrovert who sought solace in various mistresses and actively challenged any noble who seemed to compete with him for power. Sir Thomas More said of him: "He was a goodly personage and very princely to behold, of heart courageous, politic in counsel, in adversity nothing abashed . . . he was of youth greatly given to fleshy wantonness."[3] The first part of his reign had been spent in close alliance with the Earl of Warwick "The Kingmaker" to whom he owed his crown and victory over the Lancastrians; the second phase was when he found himself actively competing for absolute power with Warwick.

The latter, having more or less made Edward King, gradually became hungry for supreme power himself, but here he underestimated Edward's strength of character and tenacity of purpose. After Henry VI had been confined to the Tower and deposed, Warwick believed himself to be the most influential man in England. While Edward had secretly married Elizabeth Woodville, Anthony's sister, the Earl of Warwick was making his own plans for his sovereign's nuptials. Warwick wanted an alliance with the French which he believed would be satisfactorily negotiated if Edward could be married to Louis XI's sister-in-law. In one respect this scheme would have been useful in that it would probably have put an end to the Lancastrians obtaining support in France against the Yorkist followers of Edward. Warwick's main design was to isolate Henry VI's queen, Margaret of Anjou, from her friends at the French court. But Warwick's plan had the very real disadvantage that Louis's secret intention was to use any alliance he could obtain with England as a means of forcing her into a war with Burgundy. This would have been ruinous to England's trade with Flanders and the Netherlands.

Edward IV and Warwick were on a collision course and a showdown was inevitable. It came when, in order to put an end to Warwick's negotiations with the French, Edward confessed that he was already married. His announcement created widespread dismay and amazement at Court for Elizabeth Woodville was a widow, her husband, Sir John Grey, having been killed at the second battle of St. Albans. In medieval England there was almost an unwritten rule that a King should not marry anyone other than a virgin. Added to this was the fact that Elizabeth was a Lancastrian as well. However, Edward was a determined young man and he got his own way by having the secret marriage regularised by a service in Westminster Abbey and by extending various favours to all members of the Woodville family. Relations with Warwick were never quite the same after this and the Earl continued to pursue his policy of bringing about an alliance with France. So while Edward was seeking to seal his own alliance with Burgundy by marrying his sister Margaret to Charles the Bold, Warwick was plotting with Edward's brother, Clarence. In July, 1469, Warwick went to Calais where his brother, the Archbishop, married Warwick's elder daughter, Isobel, to Clarence.

This marked the first step in Warwick's bid for power. His intention now was to discredit Edward through Clarence and to condemn misrule by the Lancastrian-orientated "Woodville set". Certainly Edward was taken by surprise away from his capital, which had been left undefended. The Woodvilles were captured and Earl Rivers and his son, John, executed. Edward was forced temporarily to compromise with both Warwick and Clarence. For a while an uneasy truce lasted, but Edward was eventually caught at a disadvantage once again many miles from his capital. While the King was up in the north of England, Warwick who had been in France, returned, gathered an army and reached London before Edward. Queen Elizabeth, who was in London awaiting another child, sought sanctuary at Westminster with her three daughters. Edward himself, hemmed in by troops supporting Warwick as he made his dash southwards, had to escape by boat across the Wash to King's Lynn, accompanied by the new Lord Rivers, his friend Anthony Woodville. From the East Anglian port they sailed for safety in the Netherlands, seeking refuge at the Court of Burgundy.

It was even possible that Caxton may have played a part in arranging for Edward's safe arrival in the domain of Burgundy. After all he was in the employ of Edward's sister. Commines stated that Edward made his escape from the forces of the Earl of Warwick "attended by seven or eight hundred men without any clothes but what they were to have fought in, no money in their pockets, and not one in twenty of them knew whither they were going."[4]

For five months Edward remained in exile in Bruges. During all this time he seems to have made a point of winning allies in all ranks of the community by going out and about among the people. He had the common touch and was devoted to his own soldiers. Commines said that King Edward told him that "in all the battles which he had gained, his way was, when the victory was on his side, to mount on horseback, and cry out to save the common soldiers, and put the gentry to the sword." Edward was a gregarious King and this is almost certainly the period in which Caxton first met his sovereign and, by performing some services for him, paved the way to the royal patronage which he was later to enjoy in full measure.

In 1472 Edward IV granted to his sister, the Duchess of Burgundy, special privileges which enabled her to trade privately in English wool, and Caxton, as a Mercer, would have been involved in the arrangements for this. But in all his writings Caxton tells us very little indeed of his life on the continent in the earlier years. One knows he had indulged in purchasing manuscripts for other people, both in England and Flanders, but H. McCusker refers to the discovery of a manuscript in Boston, Massachusetts, which was copied in Calais and bound in northwestern Europe in the fifteenth century. A contemporary note indicates that the manuscript belonged to one William Caston and that he gave it to William Sonnyng in 1471. It is possible that Caston (or Causton) is the same as Caxton and that by this time he was already the owner of manuscripts.[5]

Edward IV had been hostile to the Hanseatic League and this no doubt had made it difficult for English merchants to deal with any Hanseatic city other than Cologne, which may explain Caxton's leanings towards that city. Cologne, together with the cities of the Netherlands, was more favourably disposed to England than the other cities of the League. It was Edward himself who largely exacerbated feeling against England among members of the League by refusing to confirm the privileges they had previously enjoyed in England and by his favouritism towards Italian merchants. There were attempts to come to some agreement, but they all dissolved in lengthy and fruitless talks. Then, in 1468, following what proved to be a false rumour of action by members of the Hanseatic League against English ships, Edward IV hastily closed the premises of the Hansards in London, imprisoned them and imposed a fine of £20,000. In January of the following year Caxton sent a long letter to the London Common Council on the subject of the Hanseatic League: no details of this are available except that it was concerned with new negotiations Caxton was undertaking in an attempt to solve the dispute. No doubt in this instance Caxton was supported by the Duke of Burgundy.

The Earl of Warwick's attempt to govern England failed because his foreign policy was not only against English interests, but opposed by the great mass of the nobles and the people. Edward had been able to strengthen the bonds with Burgundy during his exile, but, despite this, there was no enthusiasm for his return. To win some support in the north he announced that he was returning to claim the dukedom of York, not his own throne, and he made his proclamations in the name of the deposed King Henry VI. It was a wise move, for it gave him a foothold in the northern capital. On Easter Day, 1471, the Battle of Barnet was fought in swirling mists until Edward finally gained victory. In May, 1471, Edward remembered the city of Bruges which had given him refuge. Addressing a letter to the nobles and burgomasters of the city, he thanked them for their courtesy and hospitality.

By this time, at the age of only twenty-nine, Edward was in a position of enormous strength. He had proved himself in war and diplomacy, had outwitted his adversary, Warwick, and saved England from a disastrous entanglement on the continent. The country was somewhat more prosperous than when he came to the throne. The King himself had a talent for administration and he took forceful measures to put down the violence and lawlessness that had developed all over the kingdom since the Wars of the Roses. In his foreign policy he was more successful than Warwick had ever been. He gave his daughter Cecily in marriage to the heir to the Scottish throne, reconstructed the Burgundian alliance against France and the Duke of Burgundy even agreed to Edward being crowned at Rheims as "King of France".

7

The Birth of Printing

THE actual origins of printing are almost as obscure as those of Caxton himself. Probably sometime between 1380 and 1420 a primitive and secretly practised form of printing emerged in Holland; whether of Laurens Coster or others does not much matter. As Warren Chappell says: "the quality of the early Dutch type-making and printing still extant is so markedly inferior to Gutenberg's that the possibility of a few years' priority is less important than Gutenberg's results."[1]

Gutenberg was born under the name of Johann Gensfleisch in Mainz round about 1394 and he died in 1468. He was so successful as the now generally accepted inventor of printing and his craftsmanship so splendid that it is almost impossible not to believe that he had benefitted from the crude but unheralded experiments of others. On the other hand one must remember that Gutenberg was originally trained as a goldsmith which would explain how he was able to show such facility in sculpting a letter in steel. But Gutenberg must have come up against the same prejudices against printing which earlier innovators had encountered. The difference was that Gutenberg declined to be thwarted.

After all, printing was not entirely a new concept. The ancient Chinese had practised the cutting of wood blocks for a form of printing, while the Dharani Scrolls were an early specimen of wood-block printing of Japanese origin dating to the year 770. But the very idea of printing, or of reproducing in any form the work of scribes and illuminators, had been frowned upon and vetoed throughout Europe for many years. Restrictive practices were unhappily and illogically introduced in this sphere even more in the early Middle Ages than in the twentieth century. Deplorably it was often the Christian Church itself which held back the advance of culture in Europe. The monks, the calligraphers and illuminators banded together to bring pressure against anyone who proposed to duplicate their works in any form whatsoever. One suspects that laws to this effect were passed partly because these specialists wished to prevent their skill from being exploited by others at their expense, but also because the Church was not anxious for culture to be spread outside a certain narrow circle, presumably that of the Church itself and a small number of wealthy patrons of the arts. This was, of course, a reversal of the Church's role in the Dark Ages when they were fighting to preserve what culture still existed.

Apart from this the main obstacle to the development of printing was the lack of power, which was again mainly the result of restrictive practices.

It is true that a few monk-craftsmen working in monasteries began to make use of woodcuts in the latter part of the fourteenth century. A block print of St. Christopher, dated 1432, is one of the earliest examples of such work. But it was the cult of the playing-card which stimulated the development of printing in the early stages more than any other single factor. Among the goods forbidden to be imported into England in the fifteenth century were playing-cards, which had been introduced into France more than a hundred years before this Statute of Edward IV. Playing-cards became so popular that they were the recreation of working people as well as courtiers and merchants. The prohibition of their import into England was to protect their production by the natives. Various attempts had been made to ban card-playing, but without much success. The earliest cards were painted on pasteboard or plates of thin metal by using stencils, but gradually craftsmen outside the monasteries started wood-block cutting in secrecy and, of course, quite illegally. Indeed, it was only in the Venetian state that these men enjoyed any freedom to indulge in this work, and even there they were seriously restricted.

Cards were certainly printed before the middle of the fifteenth century, for there is a petition extant from the Venetian painters to their magistracy, dated 1441. This petition set out that the art of card-making and of "printing" figures, practised in Venice, had fallen into decay through the great quantity of foreign playing-cards which were being brought into the city. The Germans were the great card-makers of this period and the name by which a wood-engraver is still called in parts of Germany—a *formschneider*, occurs in the archives of Nuremberg for the year 1441.

Caxton would have seen such cards, especially at the Court of Burgundy: it is not improbable that they gave him the inspiration to explore the possibilities of printing. True, most of the playing-cards he would have seen would have been mere painted pieces of paper, but he would also have seen those produced by the stenciller in which the impressions of the engraved cards were taken off by friction.

Paper, which like primitive printing, was first developed in China, was slow in reaching the Western World in any quantity. Europe began to have paper more than a thousand years after it was invented by Ts'ai Lun in the second century. Its earliest recorded manufacture in Europe was in France in the 1430's and again at Nuremberg some fifty years later.

Thus, with the boost in paper production, there was every encouragement for Gutenberg to go ahead with his experiments. In the early days of his efforts to set up a press insufficient cash was his biggest problem. After a spell in Strasburg he returned to his native town of Mainz in 1448, borrowing some money to set up a press. A few years later he had to borrow much more and by 1455 the loans and interest had surpassed 2,000 gulden and Gutenberg was totally unable to meet his debts.

The very moment when Gutenberg had to surrender his books and tools towards paying his debts, was marked by the appearance of the Gutenberg Bible—his greatest triumph. It was one of the cultural turning points in history: within a matter of thirty years after his celebrated Gutenberg Bible was printed, printing presses in different parts of the world were turning out grammars and dictionaries.

Then in 1462 the soldiers of Adolf of Nassau, Archbishop of Mainz, attacked and looted the city of Mainz. This extraordinary example of purposeful vandalism was prompted by another development in the art of printing by one Peter Schoffer, who had devised a method by which the characters in a matrix might be singly cast instead of being cut. Schoffer was a pupil of another printer, John Fust, and the latter was so delighted with Schoffer's innovations that he promised Peter his only daughter Christina in marriage. John Schoffer, the son of Peter, who was also a printer, confirmed this story, adding that: "Fust and Schoffer concealed this new improvement by administering an oath of secrecy to all whom they entrusted, until the year 1462, when, by the dispersion of their servants into different countries, at the sacking of

Mainz by the Archbishop Adolf, the invention was publicly divulged."[2]

After the ransacking of Mainz many printers fled from the city and thus spread the invention of printing to other towns. The new art was taken up in Italy and France and in 1466 a press was set up in Cologne; within a few years printing was being carried out in Switzerland, Spain, Holland and Belgium.

Caxton would have been well aware of the development in printing in the early 'sixties even if it had not then been introduced into Belgium. It is almost certain that the idea of actually having his translations printed occurred to him at some date in the late 'sixties. His translation of the *Histories of Troy*, which Margaret of Burgundy instructed him to revise and finish and improve the style was continued in Ghent and finished in Cologne on 19 September, 1471. It is to Cologne to which we must look for Caxton's first direct contact with the world of printing.

At the end of the third book of Caxton's translation of the *Histories of Troy* he states: "Thus end I this book, which I have translated after mine author, as nigh as God hath given me cunning, to whom he given the laud and praises. And for as much as in the writing of the same my pen is worn, mine hand weary and not steadfast, mine eye even dimmed with overmuch looking on white paper, and my courage not so prone and ready to labour as it hath been, and that age creepeth on me daily and feebleth all the body; and also because I have promised to divers gentlemen and to my friends to address them as hastily as I might this said book, therefore I have practised and learned, at my great charge and expense, to ordain this said book in print, after the manner and form as you may here see; and it is not written with pen and ink as other books are, to the end that every man may have them at once. For all the books of this story named the *Recuyell of the Histories of Troy*, this imprinted as ye see here, were begun in one day, and also finished in one day. Which book I presented to my said redoubted lady as afore is said, and she hath well accepted it and largely rewarded me."

T. F. Dibdin, an early authority on Caxton, made the mistake of many of his contemporaries in taking Caxton too literally. Did Caxton mean that the book was begun and finished in one day? Did he wish his countrymen to believe that the translation of Le Fevre's book was absolutely printed in twenty-four hours? Dr. Dibdin insisted that this was impossible with a work of 778 folio pages.[3] But Caxton, writing according to the custom of his time, did not mean to imply this. He merely wished to stress the great advantage of printing—that not merely could many copies be printed at once, but that everyone might have copies at once. He does not mean that all the books were begun and finished in one day, but that all the books were begun on one day and all were finished on another day. He does not express this clearly, but it is obvious that this is what he meant.

Caxton himself told us nothing of where and how he first learned of the arts of printing. It was almost as though the subject was taboo in his time, or could it be that Caxton was rather more anxious to take credit for his printing than he was for his translation. There seems little doubt that he was heartened by the reception of his translation of *Le Recuyell* and that he decided it must be printed. It is, however, stretching the imagination too far to accept the statement published in 1664 by one Richard Atkyns that Caxton introduced printing to England in the reign of Henry VI. Atkyns based his statement on an alleged document, never produced, that asserted that: "Thomas Bourchier, Archbishop of Canterbury, moved the then King, Henry VI, to use all possible means for procuring a printing-mould . . . to be brought into this kingdom." It was further alleged that the King asked one Robert Turnour to examine the possibilities of this project and that Turnour "took to his assistance Mr. Caxton, a citizen of good abilities, who, trading much in Holland, might be a creditable pretence, as well for his going as staying in the Low Countries. Mr. Turnour was in disguise, his beard and hair shaven quite off, but Mr. Caxton appeared known and public. They, having received the sum of one thousand marks, went first to Amsterdam, then to Leyden, not daring to enter Haarlem itself; for the town was very jealous, having imprisoned and apprehended divers persons, who came from other parts for the same purpose. They staid till they had spent the whole one thousand marks in gifts and expenses. So, as the King was fain to send five hundred marks more, Mr. Turnour having written to the King that he had almost done his work, a bargain, as he said, being struck between him and two Hollanders for bringing off one of the workmen, who should sufficiently discover and teach the new art. At last, with much ado, they got off one of the under workmen, whose name was Frederick Corsells, or rather Corsellis, who late one night stole from his fellows in disguise, into a vessel prepared before for that purpose; and so the wind, favouring the design, brought him safe to London. It was not thought so prudent to set him on work at London, but by the Archbishop's means, who had been Vice-Chancellor and afterwards Chancellor of the University of Oxon, Corsellis was carried with a guard to Oxon, which constantly watched to prevent Corsellis from any possible escape, till he had made good his promise, in teaching how to print. So that at Oxford printing was first set up in England."[4]

This remarkable story has been ignored by modern biographers as being totally without foundation. Nonetheless there is in its essence an element that smacks very much of the kind of truths which are still unrevealed about Caxton's activities. In those days there was such a hush-hush attitude to printing, so much anxiety to conceal the processes on the one hand and to oppose the practice of it as dangerous on the other that the kind of cloak-and-dagger tactics which Atkyns describes are not altogether too fanciful. One can well imagine that Caxton would need to do some bribing and to have confederates skilled in espionage to enable him to bring the tools and rudiments of printing to England.

Richard Atkyns stated that "a certain worthy person did present me with a copy of a record and manuscript in Lambeth House, heretofore in his custody, belonging to the See, and not to any particular Archbishop of Canterbury. The substance whereof was this: though I hope for public satisfaction the record itself in its due time will appear." The record, despite all attempts to locate it, never has appeared.

Atkyns also stated that the same person who gave him the copy of the record trusted him with a book "printed at Oxon, A.D. 1468, which was three years before any of the recited authors would allow it [printing] to be in England." There is such a book and it is entitled *Expositio Sancti Ieronimi in Simbolum, ad Papam Laurentiam.* At the end of the book are the words *Explicit Expositio, &c, Impressa Oxonie, et finita Anno Dom. MCCCCLXVIII, XVII die Decembris.*[5]

While modern biographers of Caxton generally discard this story with scant attention, or ignore it altogether, it is nevertheless given space in Anthony Wood's *History of the University of Oxford,* and he makes the following comment: "Thus the mystery of printing appeared ten years sooner in the University of Oxford than at any other place in Europe, Haarlem and Mainz excepted. Not long after there were presses set up in Westminster, St. Alban's, Worcester and other monasteries of note. After this manner printing was introduced into England, by the care of Archbishop Bourchier, in the year of Christ, 1464, and the third of King Edward IV."

This story, though slightly more credible, is still unsubstantiated, for in 1464, with the exception of the press at Mainz and the possibility of other presses in Holland, printing was still more or less unknown in Europe. If, as Atkyns asserts, Caxton and a companion went to Haarlem in disguise to learn the art of printing, it could only have been to study the secrets of the still almost legendary Coster. But if the stories—admittedly wholly unsubstantiated—about Coster are true, then Caxton would have had to go to Haarlem before 1442, as by this date Coster is reputed to have been robbed of his secret printing processes, all his types and tools. On the other hand if Atkyns was relying on second-hand information, it may be that he was misinformed about Haarlem and that Caxton possibly went to Mainz.

Most critics denounce Atkyns as a fraud and suggest that he invented this story about Caxton. Dr. Conyers Middleton bluntly commented in this respect that Atkyns was: "a bold, vain man, might be the inventor of it, having an interest in imposing upon the world, to confirm his argument that printing was of the prerogative royal, in opposition to stationers, against whom he was engaged in expensive law-suits, in defence of the King's patents, under which he claimed some exclusive powers of printing."[6]

This is a somewhat harsh judgement and a sweeping assertion. If Atkyns wished to invent such a story, he could have done so with greater credibility and even some documentary evidence, if he had linked Caxton's name with Edward IV and suggested that the King took the initiative in bringing printing to England. For whereas there are documents showing that Caxton received money from Edward IV, there is no record of Henry VI having provided funds for him. What is of interest is that the story of Coster's experiments was known in England when Caxton was still an apprentice to Robert Large—within a year of Henry VI founding Eton. This scholarly King, one of the few intellectuals who have sat on the throne of England, would have been fascinated by reports of the invention of printing and it would have been wholly in character for him to have sought Caxton's assistance in obtaining a press. The fact that there is no evidence for this should not be taken as final. It is merely that Atkyns' story is unproven and probably, taking a benevolent view of his testimony, based on half-accurate information and confusion of dates and places. As to the date of 1468 on the Oxford book, this is almost certainly a typographical error. It is a well printed book for the period and the same type and manner of printing are to be seen in books printed at Oxford after 1478. Somehow a Roman numeral must have been omitted in the date line.

That Caxton was aware of printing experiments going on in Europe at an early stage is shown in what he wrote himself in his continuation of the *Polychronicon*: "About this time [1455] the craft of imprinting was first found in Mogunce in Almayne." One must assume that this refers to Mainz in Germany. The French for Mainz was *Mayence*, while the city itself was founded in 13 B.C. as Drusus as "Maguntiacum". With the English passion for shortening words and names, it is easy to see how Mogunce was arrived at. From his vantage point at the Court of Burgundy Caxton would not only hear reports of the development of printing, but see specimens of the craft. Bruges was a focal point of culture. Therefore it is almost certain that the idea of printing books was uppermost in his mind several years before he actually set out to obtain a press. Maybe this interest dated to the reign of Henry VI. N. F. Blake writes that Caxton's decision to learn how to print may be dated to 1 March, 1469, when he began the translation *The Histories of Troy*. It was part of the grand design of learning how to print.[7]

Now the implication here is clear—that Caxton persevered with translations only because ultimately he wanted to print books. What were his motives? Was it that he foresaw the revolutionary possibilities opened up by printing? Was it that he wanted to see books produced in the English language? Or was it that as a merchant he saw the commercial possibilities of obtaining a press and acquiring something like a monopoly for printing books in England and making money that way? Most likely it was a combination of all these things. It has been pointed out that all the books commissioned by Margaret of Burgundy were in French and that it would be unlikely that it was for her sake that he produced a printed book in English. But, as an Englishwoman, there is no doubt that she would and did encourage him to make these translations. It was in the interest of her brother, Edward IV. Of course there is no doubt whatsoever that Caxton, both as a Mercer and as

Governor of the English Nation, would realise that anyone introducing printing to England would automatically obtain a monopoly and a stranglehold on the whole market. But it would be unkind to suggest he was influenced solely by mercenary motives. Indeed, when one considers the risks continental printers underwent, whether concerning the legendary Coster or the well documented Gutenberg, it would be ridiculous to suggest that anyone chanced his arm in these early days of printing just for the money.

It is clear that Caxton had a passion for the English language, for developing it and for changing it from a hotchpotch of dialects to a cohesive, expressive force. Despite the lack of information we have about him, his own words bear this out again and again. Why else did he impose on the English language in translation, French words that he thought would improve it and embellish the development of English? There is no evidence that Caxton received any help or backing in the early years for his printing projects, either in the Court of Burgundy or in London. Such aid may have been forthcoming, but we have no proof of it. On the other hand we have proof that Caxton cared about the English language—to cite only his own words. What emerges from what he wrote is that he cared intensely about the English language and was worried about the indeterminate condition into which it had been allowed to fall. It is argued that Caxton's education is a matter of conjecture, that he was not a scholar and therefore could not possibly be either a good translator, or know anything about literature. This is, of course, total nonsense. Literature in England has always had its main roots deep in the lower middle classes from John Lydgate to Dylan Thomas. A hippie monk and a hard-drinking Welshman deeply immersed in conjuring with words have shown how English can be developed: so, too, did Daniel Defoe, Dickens, Thomas Hardy and others from the lower middle class. It was at Cologne where Caxton first saw a printing press and learned about the art. Whether or not he still had official connections with England then one cannot be sure. It is clear that he was in Cologne by 17 July, 1471, though he made no statement about learning the art of printing there. Yet the earlier biographers of Caxton continued to doubt that he learned about printing in Cologne. There is evidence that while in Cologne he had dealings with various authorities and merchants concerning negotiations for commercial treaties connected with the Hanseatic League.

There are, too, the words of Wynkyn de Worde's *De Proprietatibus Rerum* (Bartholomeus Anglicus), printed in 1495:

> "And also of your charity call to remembrance
> The soul of William Caxton, first printer of this book
> In Latin tongue at Cologne, himself to advance,
> That every well-disposed man may thereon look;
> And John Tate the younger joy mote he brook,
> Which late hath in England do make this paper thin,
> That now in English this book is printed in."[8]

The reference to Tate is, incidentally, the earliest record of the name of any English paper-maker. This quotation is evidence that Caxton learned his art in Cologne, but has previously been discounted as an error. A Latin edition of the *De Proprietatibus Rerum* exists, lacking the printer's name, place or date of printing, but it is now established to have been the work of an anonymous Cologne printer styled as "The Printer of the *Flores Sancti Augustini*" after one of his books. The only dated book printed by this press is 1473, while Caxton is known to have been in Cologne in September, 1471. All doubts about Caxton's associations with Cologne in this vital period are removed by the researches of Dr. Henry Thomas, Deputy Keeper of the Printed Books, British Museum, in his *Wilh. Caxton uyss Engelant* published in an edition of 200 copies at Cologne in 1928.[9]

The absolute proof of Caxton having been in Cologne in the period mentioned is contained in the Cologne Aliens' Register:

> "(i) *Mercurij xvij Julij* (1471)
> *Wilh. Caxton uyss engelant ad mensen*
> *cum resignatione iij dierum.*
>
> (ii) *Veneris Nona Augusti* (1471)
> *Wilhelm Kaxston usque nativitatis christi cum resignatione*
> *8 dierum.*
>
> (iii) *Mercurij Xj x bris*
> *Wilhelm Kaxsum uyss Engelant usque*
> *Johannis Baptiste ut supra cum resignatione viij dierum.*
>
> (iv) *Veneris xix Junij* (1472)
> *Wilhelm Kaxton uyss Engelant continuatis ut*
> *supra ad medium annum cum resignatione*
> *viij dierum.*"

To sum up, Caxton was in Cologne two months earlier than the date he gives in his preface, having leave to stay for a month, subject to three days' notice of withdrawal. Permission to stay in Cologne was three times renewed, subject to eight days' notice, and successive renewals point to some special reason for his stay in the city. It is clear that he was there throughout the time in which the *editio princeps* of the *DPR* was being printed. In other words one can accept the testimony of Wynkyn de Worde.

It is possible therefore that Caxton left Cologne during the latter part of 1472 to spend a few years in the Netherlands, setting up his own press in Bruges. Holbrook Jackson takes an extremely dispassionate view of Caxton in trying to reconstruct his attitude to printing. Jackson writes that: "it is evident also that he [Caxton] paid little or no attention in the early stages of his enterprise to the aesthetics of the new craft. The probable explanation of this is that he felt, unconsciously no doubt, that unaffected printing best suited plain language. He was probably interested in becoming a plain and practical printer rather than a stylish printer, hoping, perchance, that his vernacular books would look their part and not ape the aristocratic manners of the then fashionable Latin classics, Bibles and liturgical books."[10]

This is hardly borne out by any careful analysis of Caxton's printed works, or of what he wrote about them. It is as slick and uninformed a judgement as any of those earlier writers on Caxton who tried to build him up into something approaching the chief scholar of the century. Everything we know about Caxton points to the fact that he was fully conscious of the need for a revolution in the English language and that, unless this could be achieved with an influx of French words and phrases, it would not come up to the standards of the European courts. Caxton was a professional, or at least in the course of time he made himself a professional in that he edited what he printed for a specific market. It is worth mentioning that Caxton's versatility as a printer ranged from the printing of Indulgences and pamphlets to lengthy romances and that he was always experimenting with new types. Holbrook Jackson's further comment is that: "whatever faults his typography possessed were outweighed by that honesty of purpose by means of which he opened the way to the building of a great common language for his fellow countrymen. The very fact that he was a man of sound sense and general intelligence rather than a highly specialised scholar helped him in his task and assured his success." This second opinion somewhat cuts across his first thesis, but the whole point that Holbrook Jackson seems to have missed is Caxton's professionalism in his approach to his work and in his printing. To talk about faults in typography in the earliest days of printing is academic quibbling.

It seems probable that Caxton learned the art of printing from one Ulrich Zell, a priest from Mainz who established the first press in Cologne. Possibly Caxton was informed of Zell's activities through his own intelligence system. In those days anyone holding Caxton's position would be almost automatically held responsible for obtaining intelligence for his country.

Cologne was the nearest city to Bruges to have a press of its own at this time and it was in its way a cultural centre, having a university and an extensive trade with England. The merchants of Cologne were well disposed towards England, having their own colony in London. Caxton would obviously have taken full advantage of this, strengthening relationships between the two cities. The Cologne merchants had maintained a lengthy trade relationship with England and this included the exporting of books.

From 1461 to 1470 the presses of Mainz, Bamberg, Cologne and Strasburg had produced Latin and German Bibles, while in the same period the Italian presses in Milan, Rome and Venice had also printed classical works. The art had made such rapid progress in Italy that in the first edition of St. Jerome's Epistles, printed in 1468, the Bishop of Almeria addressed Pope Paul II thus: "It was reserved for the times of your holiness for the Christian world to be blessed with the immense advantages of printing, by means of which, and with a little money, the poorest person may collect together a few books. It is a small testimony of the glory of your holiness that the volumes which formerly scarcely an hundred golden crowns would purchase, may now be procured for twenty and less, and these well written and authentic ones." It was precisely this kind of message which got through to Caxton and inspired in him a professional approach to the task of printing and, more important, popularising what was printed.

Caxton certainly used a type which was based on a type-style of script used in the areas around the Rhine. Zell, who had passed out of the University of Cologne in June, 1464, was a natural model for the Englishman. Zell started printing somewhat later than this, linking up with the Mainz printers and acquiring a press of his own. Paper was then the biggest problem for printers, as indeed it is today. The successful printer needed to acquire ample quantities of paper. Zell seems to have succeeded more than most and for this reason he would have been the one to whom Caxton was likeliest to turn. But in the case of Zell it is probable that the financing of his printing projects came from a religious order. It has been suggested that this order was that of the Brothers of the Common Life at Weidenbach in Cologne, though there is no evidence that Caxton associated with the Brothers.[11]

Possibly Caxton became associated with the Brothers as a merchant and exporter of books. Possibly in the first stages of his relationship with them he sold books which they produced. What is clear is that the press from which he learned printing in Cologne used a type utilising the Brothers' script. One must remember that Caxton was deeply religious and that, when away from his base, he would be likely to associate with religious orders, preferring to share in the monastic life which was similar to that of his earlier days in the *Domus Anglorum*. When he was in Ghent he stayed with the Benedictines and when in Cologne he probably stayed with another order. But it was in Cologne that he turned himself into a professional printer, not merely by study-ing the techniques of local printers, but by understanding what their marketing possibilities were. He was always much more conscious of the need to find an adequate market for printed books than were most of the early printers. It was Caxton the merchant, Caxton the salesman who really projected Caxton the printer.

In Cologne he learned the complete art of printing from the putting of type into a composing stick to handling the paper and working the press. Though he saw himself as a planner and distributor of books rather than a printer, he understood that he would need to learn the craft if only to be able to train apprentices when he returned to England. For everything points to the fact that Caxton had planned to introduce printing to England before he went to Cologne.

Blades suggested that Caxton learned his art in the Netherlands—a theory which brings us back to Henry VI and Coster—arguing that otherwise his printing would have been better than it was. But these faults—for example, the uneven line endings—were also present in a good deal of German work, notably the work of the *Flores Sancti Augustini*. His chief assistant in Cologne was undoubtedly Wynkyn de

Worde, an Alsatian from Wörth, who appears to have been an un-enterprising printer who, while following Caxton to London, did little other than copy his master's work. But he seems to have been a loyal servant and to have made himself almost indispensable to Caxton.

As far as we can tell Caxton left Cologne in 1472 and returned to Bruges, where he set up his own press. He obviously wanted to be quite sure he could master the technique of printing before he returned to London and he felt that the next stage was to experiment in Bruges. Everything points to the fact that Caxton had first printed in Cologne and that he undertook the Latin edition of Bartholomaeus as a commercial speculation. But Caxton had learned at first hand of the many set-backs and the terrible disasters which had beset even the most skilled and ardent of printers. He was determined to learn about all the snags before he chanced his luck in England. First he needed to win further patronage from the Duchess of Burgundy and, through her influence in England, to pave the way for his own press there. *The Histories of Troy*, in which she had already shown a keen interest, was a natural choice for his first printed work. The work itself carries neither the date nor the place of publication, but it probably came out in 1473–4. It was a large work and would possibly have taken several months to produce. One must assume that this book was printed in Bruges shortly after he returned there from Cologne.

To ensure success Caxton sought the services of another assistant in Bruges, this time of a calligrapher named Colard Mansion, who, in collaboration with Caxton, produced a type that was a discursive gothic, based on Fleming script and of a style that became known as *bâtarde*. Mansion was not merely a highly regarded professional scribe, but also a bookseller in Bruges, so, from Caxton's point of view, he had the talent of a type designer and a knowledge of markets. M. J. P. A. Madden thinks that Caxton and Colard Mansion were students of printing together in Cologne in 1471–4.

Printing was still a highly precarious occupation and Caxton must have needed considerable diplomacy to get his press going. Without the Burgundian Court it is doubtful whether he would ever have succeeded sufficiently to introduce printing to England. Lambinet, a French bibliographical writer, told how Melchior de Stamham, when setting up a press at Augsburg, engaged a skilled craftsman named Sauerloch with whom he bought five presses and from the materials of

Caxton and his press, from a painting by Vivian Forbes. (*Radio Times*)

these he constructed five other presses. He cast pewter types and, having spent a vast sum in setting up his printing works, he began work in 1473. But Sauerloch died, broken-hearted, before he had finished one single book, and even this unfinished work was sold off for a trifling sum and his presses were broken up. Melchior de Stamham simply had no more money left to carry on. Such was the fate of many of the earlier printers.

Caxton would have had to encounter similar problems and one must assume that his experience as both diplomat and merchant enabled him to survive where others had failed. Despite all the theories of modern printing experts on the subject of Caxton, one cannot do better than quote Charles Knight, writing in the early nineteenth century on this subject. He says that the early printers: "had to do everything for themselves; to construct the materials of their art, types, presses and every other instrument and appliance. When Caxton began to print at Cologne, he probably had the means of obtaining a set of moulds from some previous printer—what are called strikes from the punches that form the original matrices. The writers upon typography seem to assume the necessity of every one of the old printers cutting his punches anew, and shaping his letters according to his own notions of proportionate beauty. That the great masters of their art, the first inventors, the Italian printers, the Alduses, the Stephenses, pursued this course is perfectly clear. But when printing ceased to be a mystery about 1462, it is more than probable that those who tried to set up a press, especially in Germany, either bought a few types of the more established printers, or obtained a readier means of casting types than that of cutting new punches—a difficult and expensive operation. . . . But the type obtained, Caxton would still have much to do before his office was furnished."[12]

This gives a fairly clear picture of the obstacles Caxton had to overcome before he could risk coming to England. So many early experiments ended in total disaster. In the case of Melchior de Stamham, when, according to contemporary reports, it is stated that he bought five presses and turned them into new presses, what is almost certainly meant is that he purchased five old wine presses, and, using the screws, cut them down and adapted them for printing. Some of the earliest printing presses were little more than adapted common screw-presses such as a cheese-press or a napkin-press, with a gadget for running the form of types under the screw after the form was inked. This would have been a slow and laborious process, providing the printer with little hope of quick profits to recoup the considerable outlay he would have had to make.

Printing, in these early days, was fraught with frightening risks, and failures were more frequent than successes. Caxton would have needed not merely to master the arts of printing, but of ink-making as well, and to ensure that he had ready access to quantities of paper. Only a professional merchant could have succeeded in these uncharted seas of obvious and still unseen hazards.

8

Return to England

IT can fairly be assumed that Caxton and Colard Mansion were more or less equals in the world of printing and not that, as William Blades suggested, Caxton depended on Mansion. Each had something to contribute to the new art, but there is little doubt that Caxton was the senior partner.

This was the partnership which produced probably, as already said, in 1474 at Bruges the first book printed in the English language, *The Histories of Troy*, and for two years after this the two men worked closely together. The French translation of *Le Recueil des Histoires de Troye*, from which Caxton worked, was the composition of Raoul Lefevre, the chaplain and secretary to the former Duke of Burgundy, Philip the Good. Then Caxton studied a French translation of *Liber de Ludo Scachorum*, by J. de Cessolis, in which the game of chess was likened to that of life itself. Fascinated by the comparison and the lessons posed by it, Caxton decided that more Englishmen should learn how to play this game, but, to give it that touch of piety which he could never resist, the printer gave his translation the title of *The Game and Play of the Chess Moralised*, dedicating it curiously enough not to his royal master, Edward IV, but to the King's recent enemy, the Duke of Clarence. Here the cautious merchant may have been anxious to hedge his bets: the eventual outcome of the power struggle in England was far from certain and Edward had been magnanimous to Clarence in receiving him back with warmth and allowing him to resume his office of Lord Lieutenant of Ireland. There is also evidence that Clarence was a great favourite of the Duchess of Burgundy, which may have influenced Caxton's choice for the dedication. He no longer held an official position in the English community in Bruges: his whole future was bound up in his printing projects and he needed to have the maximum amount of support.

Yet the selection of this book on chess seems to have been entirely his own, and indeed in his preface to it he referred to himself as being "unknown" to the royal personage to whom he had dedicated it. But though Caxton held no official position on the English side, he appears to have undertaken some discreet diplomatic negotiations even if these are cloaked in obscurity. They were mainly connected with the Hanseatic League and commercial terms to be arranged between the Court of Burgundy and England.

This second book of Caxton's was once again undated, but it was most probably printed by Colard's press in 1475. Caxton wrote in a later edition of the book that "I did do set [it] in imprinte", by which he was referring not to his having set the type for the book, but that he "caused" it to be printed.

There is an interesting sidelight on Caxton's attitude to lawyers which the printer worked into the text of this work. It would seem that he must have suffered himself from lawyers at some time or other, for he writes: ". . . in England what hurt do the advocates, men of law and attorneys of court to the common people of the royaume, as well in the spiritual law as in the temporal: how turn they the law and statutes at their pleasure; how eat they the people, how impoverish they the community. I suppose that in all Christendom are not so many pleaders, attorneys and men of the law as be in England, only, for if they were numbered all that long to the courts of the Chancery, King's Bench, Common Pleas, Exchequer, Receipt and Hall, and the bag-bearers of the same, it should amount to a great multitude. And how all these live and of whom, if it should not be uttered and told it should not be believed. For they extend to their singular weal and profit and not to the common."

Caxton's other book produced in Bruges in 1476 was the *Quatres Derrenières Choses* which he and Mansion produced together, and it marked the first occasion in which Caxton tried out a new fount of type, that afterwards known as type two. Once again the book was produced without either the printers' names, date or place of production. An important departure in printing this book was the use of red ink for the title-lines.

Proof corrections must have been one of the more exasperating chores of all in this early printing. Usually a scholar was employed to read proofs and check things over and, when confronted with careless type-setting, there must have been many angry moments. Caxton was almost certainly his own proof corrector and this would save him time and anguish, not to mention furious disputes with scholars who failed to understand how easy it was for a printer to get his letters mixed up. On the accuracy of the type-setting and the patience of the proof corrector much depended: Caxton has something to say about this in an oblique sense in one work. It is generally understood that Caxton was so cautious a printer that he required an assurance that he could sell enough of any one book to pay the cost of producing it. "If I have submitted myself to translate into English the *Legend of Saints*", he wrote in his preface to this book, ". . . and William, Earl of Arundel, desired me—and promised to take a reasonable quantity of them—and sent me a worshipful gentleman, promising that my said lord should during my life give and grant me a yearly fee, that is to note, a buck in summer and a doe in winter."[1] Caxton seems to have displayed far more business acumen than any other of these early printers, for an arrangement such as the one just mentioned was far in excess of anything most of them could have hoped for. Conrad Sweyheym and Arnold Pannartz, the Germans who introduced printing to Italy in 1465, when presenting a petition to the Pope in 1471, reminding him that they were the first to introduce their art into his territories "with vast labour and cost", added that "if you peruse the catalogue of the works printed by us, you will admire how and where we could procure a sufficient quantity of paper, or even rags, for such a number of volumes. The total of these books amounts to 12,475—a prodigious hoard—and intolerable to us, your Holiness's printers, by reason of those unsold. We are no longer able to bear the great expense of housekeeping, for want of buyers, of which there cannot be more flagrant proof than that our house, though otherwise spacious enough, is full of quire-books, but void of every necessary of life."[2]

Some of the evidence of Caxton's sagacity and caution, his husbanding of his resources and his keen eye for sales, has been cited by critics to suggest he was only motivated by commercial instincts. This is surely grossly unfair and is as much an overreaction by modern critics as was that of those of earlier centuries who patriotically but fulsomely tried to build Caxton up into a master-mind in the world of literature. All printers took some risk in attempting to use this new medium at all. In Caxton's case he tried to minimise those risks by applying his experience in business to the trade of a printer and it is a measure of his

determination and calibre that he set about these things more profes-
sionally than most. In reply to such carping critics it is worth noting
that the volume of what one might call his "commercial printing" was
far smaller than his literary printing. True, he relied on patronage to a
large extent, but then this was the custom of the times. And patronage
was not all that it seemed to be. Occasionally patrons suggested books
and paid the expenses of having them produced. More often they paid
only a small portion of such expenses and the printer was still left with
the problem of selling the books. But sometimes the patron was totally
unaware of his patronage: in short, his name was used for prestige
purposes, or in the hope that it would sell the book. It is almost certain
that the Duke of Clarence never met Caxton and knew nothing whatsoever about the book the printer dedicated to him. But the name of
Clarence would carry weight in Court circles and this indirectly would
aid Caxton's cause.

The "commercial printing" undertaken by Caxton included Statutes
produced for sale to lawyers, Indulgences and vocabulary and phrase
books. Possibly, too, some minor works for the use of the clergy would
come into this category. But the vast majority of Caxton's books and
works comes under the heading of translated literature, even, perhaps,
when it came to his work in editing some of the English poets. Here
Caxton had a special problem: on the continent, as Curt F. Buhler has
pointed out, the linguistic changes from medieval to modern pro-
nunciation had preceded the appearance of the press, whereas in
England it was printing which had to "fix" the orthography of the
language which was still in a state of flux.[3] Thus Caxton was at one
and the same time translator, editor, shaper of the English language
and printer. Without being a printer he could never have succeeded in
his other roles, but who can say with certainty in which role he excelled?

Almost certainly other factors than his desire to develop printing
caused Caxton's return to England. Relations between Burgundy and
England had begun to grow sour after a promising start and the constant warmongering of the Duke of Burgundy and the decline in trade
probably led to Caxton's decision to leave Bruges. It was as well he
left when he did for in 1477 Charles the Bold was killed in battle and
the Duchy of Burgundy was annexed by France.

It was in the autumn of 1476 that Caxton returned to England to set up as a printer. An entry in the rent-roll of John Esteney, Sacrist of Westminster Abbey, for the year beginning 29 September, 1476, and ending on 28 September, 1477, records that *"De alia shopa ibidem dismisso Willelmo Caxton, X⁸*, [For another shop in the same let to William Caxton, 10 shillings]. It will be noted that no actual date is given for the taking up of the let, but it would seem certain that it was either at the end of September, or early in October, 1476, that Caxton came here, as the first piece of printing by him in England was clearly dated 13 December, 1476. This was the Letter of Indulgence issued by John Sant, Abbot of Abingdon, to Henry Lanley (or Langley), of London, and Katherine, his wife. Indulgences were pardons granted by the Church, giving sinners absolution from their sins; the sinner had to buy the pardon from the Church at an agreed price. This Indulgence could only have been issued at Westminster about two months after Caxton set up his press. It was found in the Public Record Office in 1928 and is the earliest surviving item of printing in England. The type face used was one recognised as Caxton's: it is almost indistinguishable from manuscript work, as will be seen by carefully comparing the actual typeface with words written into the certificate. The last word "Sexto" in the Indulgence and insertions on the two preceding lines and the third line from the top are handwritten. It is extremely difficult to tell the difference.

About seventy years ago Dr. Edward J. L. Scott, Keeper of the Manuscripts and Egerton Library at the British Museum, gave details of the existence of new material concerning Caxton among the Muniments at Westminster Abbey. This comprised nearly 350 documents relating to the Causton or Caxton family and their lands at Edmonton, Enfield and Tottenham in the fourteenth century, together with a series of entries in the account rolls of the Prior, Sacrist and Almoner of Westminster Abbey. The latter recorded the payment of rent by Caxton himself and his successor, Wynkyn de Worde, for the houses they occupied between the years 1477 and 1499.

But the Causton and Caxton documents are still somewhat of a mystery. They do not help in any way to establish the identity of Caxton's ancestors and reveal no link with the printer, though they do show that a certain William de Causton, who died in 1354, was a member of the Mercers' Company, and that—to cite Lawrence E. Tanner, Keeper of the Muniments, Westminster Abbey—"it is also

Caxton's house in Westminster. (*Radio Times*)

not without significance that Caxton's father was living in Westminster when his son set up his printing-press in the precincts, and that a certain Richard Caxton, who there is reason to believe was a relative of the printer, was one of our monks from 1473 to 1502."[4]

I find these statements somewhat categorical about the possibility of relationships with the printer, Caxton. They certainly induce some interesting speculation and it is more than likely that Richard Caxton was a relative, possibly a nephew. The fact remains however that it is baffling as to why these documents should ever have come to be among the Abbey Muniments because the properties to which they refer were never owned by the Abbot and Convent of Westminster. There are two possibilities. It may have been, as sometimes often happens, that, when a man has been away from his own country for a long period, he takes a special interest in tracing his family connections. Though there is no evidence that Caxton was interested either in his own or other people's family trees, it may well have been so. Alternatively these documents may have been in the possession of the monk, Richard Caxton, who left them to the Abbey Muniments when he died.

Early biographers of Caxton tended to make guesses as to the actual site and description of the building where Caxton first set up as a printer. It was known that his printing premises or shop bore the heraldic sign of the "Red Pale", but it was not generally realised that he did not open his premises there until about 1482–3, so that, contrary to what his earlier biographers asserted, his first shop was not in the Almonry of Westminster Abbey, as had been almost unanimously maintained for many years.

Despite the record of his setting up a shop in Westminster in about the early autumn of 1476, it still cannot be said for certain where this was situated, but it must have been close to the Chapter House of Westminster Abbey on the left hand side of the path leading to the south or Poets' Corner door. Books printed in this first shop of Caxton's have been inscribed as having been "emprynted by me, William Caxton, in the Abbey of Westminster", whereas the later books printed in the Almonry just have the inscription of "at Westminster".

It was in November, 1954, when a memorial tablet referring to William Caxton was unveiled outside the south or Poets' Corner door of Westminster Abbey to commemorate the assistance given by the Press to the successful Abbey Appeal Fund for £1,000,000, that Lawrence E. Tanner re-examined the question of the location of Caxton's first printing shop. He worked on the researches of Dr. Edward Scott and Mr. W. J. L. Crotch and, as a result, was able to correct certain mistakes made by earlier biographers.[5] It soon became clear that the site of the shop was near to the east end of the Abbey and Old Palace Yard, an area in which Caxton's own hero, Geoffrey Chaucer, had himself lived and which was still standing when Caxton came to Westminster.

The nearest we have to an accurate description of the site of Caxton's original printing works comes from Lawrence Tanner, so his statement on the subject is of the utmost importance. "On the other side of the Chapel [the Old Lady Chapel] there was a large house

WESTMINSTER ABBEY

GREAT
CLOISTER

1

SITE OF
ST ALBANS
HOUSE

3

4

DEAN'S
YARD

COLLEGE GARDEN

1 The Chapter House
2 Caxton's first shop
3 The Almonary
4 Caxton's second house

The precincts of Westminster Abbey in Caxton's time, showing the site of his premises.

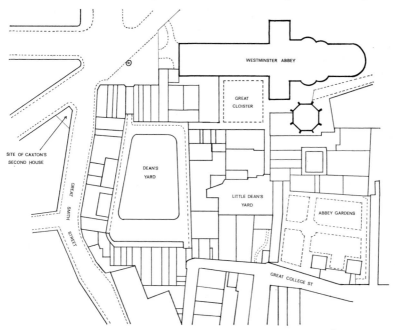

WESTMINSTER ABBEY

GREAT
CLOISTER

SITE OF CAXTON'S
SECOND HOUSE

DEAN'S
YARD

LITTLE DEAN'S
YARD

ABBEY GARDENS

GREAT SMITH STREET

GREAT COLLEGE ST

A modern map of the Abbey precincts.

enclosed within stone walls called St. Albans. It filled most of the space covered by the green to the east of the Chapter House where now stands the statue of King George V. There is nothing in our records to show how this house obtained its name. It first appears among the rents in the Sacrist's Account Roll for 1473–1474. It was then in the tenure of William and Joan Stowell who had it on a term of forty years of which that year was the second—the roll for 1472–1473 is missing. They were the parents of Robert Stowell, the master mason of the Abbey. After the death of his father in 1476 Robert Stowell went to live with his mother and he is known to have been a friend of Caxton and his family. The house was an important one, and in one form or another, although later it was divided up into separate houses and probably largely if not entirely rebuilt, it did not finally disappear until the 1890's, although the old name of St. Albans fades out in the middle of the eighteenth century. Among its later tenants were Lord Beauchamp of Powicke, Lord Shrewsbury, William Cecil, the great Lord Burghley, and Sir Randolph Crewe.

"Between St. Albans and the Abbey there was, and is, a road or path leading from Old Palace Yard to the south or Poet's Corner door of the Abbey which is now spanned at its west end by one of the flying buttresses of the Chapter House. It is with this road or path that we shall be concerned. . . .

". . . It was clear to Mr. Crotch and myself that Caxton did not set up the original printing-press in the Almonry, as had been asserted over and over again by previous writers, but elsewhere in the precincts and that it was not until some years later, either in 1482 or 1483, that he took in addition to his original shop the premises in the Almonry usually known as the Red Pale. But we were not able to give the exact site of this first shop, and the only clues we had were first the presumption that it was probably somewhere near St. Albans, and secondly that the first of the shops mentioned in 1476–1477 was described in a later account roll for 1488–1489 as being next to the Glass House or *juxta la logge vitrarius.*"[6]

This was the nearest to a vital clue. Research into the Sacrist's Account Rolls after Caxton died showed that Wynkyn de Worde paid rent for Caxton's old shop until 1499–1500, after which he moved to Fleet Street. It was in this year that the "next door shop next the glass house" was let to one James Bookbynder. He stayed there until 1508–

1509 when, in the records the usual description of the premises as being "next the glass house" is no longer used, but when the shop is let to one John Elys it is designated as the shop annexed to the Chapter House and later still, in 1530, as the shop "lying next to the south door of the Church".

From all this Lawrence Tanner deduced that the first Caxton printing-press was set up in a house adjoining to or close to the Chapter House, on the left-hand side of the path leading to the south or Poets' Corner door, and that the shop was more or less associated with book production until 1531–1532. Tanner also makes the point that: "if, as is possible, one of the other shops which Caxton rented on the site was on the opposite side of the path it would have nestled under the Chapels of St. Edmund or St. Nicholas, and here perhaps we have the real explanation of the term 'chapel' which is so familiar in the printing trade."[7] The word "chapel" is now much more associated with trade unionism in the newspaper world than it is in any other sphere of life. But I hardly think this can be linked with Caxton. I doubt, too, whether it can be linked even with his assistant, Wynkyn de Worde, who eventually went to Fleet Street and so founded the traditions of the British press. Writing of the history of St. Bride's Church in Fleet Street, Dewi Morgan says that: "it was because medieval churchmen clustered around this bank of the Fleet Ditch that Wynkyn de Worde brought Caxton's press to Fleet Street . . . Thus did the life of St. Bride's become a singular thread in the tapestry of the history of English letters and therefore of English life."[8] It is mere romantic speculation to suggest that the origin of the trade union chapel, whether of printers' or journalists' unions lies in Caxton's, or Wynkyn de Worde's ecclesiastical connections. The stark truth is that trade unionism generally sprang out of the chapel of Nonconformity— the chapel of religious dissension and opposition to the Establishment —not the chapel of either the Catholic or Anglican Churches. It is nevertheless ironical that even modern Marxists insist on using the mystique of the word "chapel" to preserve its sanctity and to give the title of "Father of the Chapel" to the chairman of the committee, this imposing a kind of bogus consecration on members. Such is the innate conservatism of trade union members that none of them, moderate or revolutionary, has never tried to abolish this wholly ridiculous nomenclature of "chapel" and "father".

Caxton may have had many reasons for settling in this shop near the Chapter House. Possibly he had relatives in the vicinity, but a more important reason would certainly be that this site was close to the seat of English Government and within easy reach of his patrons or hoped-for patrons. The Palace of Westminster was both the King's residence and the seat of government and this adjoined the Abbey. The Palace comprised the Exchequer Hall, the Star Chamber, the Queen's Hall, nursery, King's Wardrobe, Chandlery and Almonry. Surrounding it were gardens and orchards, fishponds and granaries and vineries, giving Westminster an almost rustic aura. Closer to the River Thames were barracks, stables and barns, while the Abbey itself housed some 400 people, additional to its eighty monks.

There is a record in the Abbey Muniments that Caxton paid 4d. for a shop which he rented for a week "in time of the Parliament" in 1488–1489. At that period, and until the year 1540, the normal meeting place for the House of Commons was the Westminster Chapter House, and, as Lawrence Tanner points out: "the most direct and indeed the obvious way for the constant coming and going that there must have been between the Chapter House and the Palace (where the Lords sat) was through the south transept of the Church and the south or Poets' Corner door and so past Caxton's shop and booth."[9] There could hardly have been a better site for a bookshop in London in those days and it is not surprising that Caxton kept it on, presumably simply as a shop, even after he moved his press to larger premises in the Almonry.[10]

Anyone embarking on so ambitious a project as the introduction of printing into England at this period would need to be within easy reach of patrons and potential patrons, customers who could afford to buy books and those who would give some protection to one practising a trade which was still suspected by some as being "a contraption of the Devil". Westminster was not only an admirable site for the reasons already mentioned, but because, by setting up his press in the shadows of the Abbey and its precincts, Caxton was indirectly giving himself the benefit of ecclesiastical protection and approval, if not patronage. He was obviously on the best of terms with the Abbey authorities, a most useful qualification for his right to print which, in those days of Guild rivalry, might very easily have been challenged. Susan Cunnington rightly points out that in settling in Westminster Caxton's chief reason probably was that: "in this powerful shelter and gracious centre of learning, he would be free from vexatious restrictions and trade jealousies."[11] That such restrictions existed is clear from the fact that opponents of the arts of printing included the writers and scriveners who formed so large a part of the Guild of Stationers. Caxton was not a member of that Guild, which was all powerful in the City of London, and it could well have been that had he set up his printing press within the boundaries of the City, the Stationers would have laid a complaint against him to the Lord Mayor and sought to ban him from using his press there. As Henry R. Plomer says, the Guild of Stationers "may well have thought, as . . . most of the clergy did, that it [printing] was an unholy thing and savoured of the devil. . . . But at Westminster Caxton was outside the jurisdiction of the City, and under the shadow of the Abbey could do pretty much as he liked."[12]

To win the permission, or at least the tacit approval of the clergy, Caxton must have been on extremely good terms with those in authority at the Abbey, or had good friends in high places. There is no reason to think that he had any patrons among the clergy at the Abbey and there is no indication that he was employed in any way by the Abbot. His output of service-books was small. But Canon Benet Burgh, of the Chapel of St. Stephens, may well have put a certain amount of printing in his way and we do know that he gave Caxton his own translation of *Caton*, which was printed about 1484, and of which Caxton wrote that it "hath been translated into English by Mayster Benet Burgh, late Archdeacon of Colchester and Canon of St. Stephens at Westminster, which full craftily hath made it in a ballad royal for the education of my lord Bouchier, son and heir of the Earl of Essex."

E. Gordon Duff suggests that Caxton chose the vicinity of Westminster Abbey as a site for his printing press because this vicinity was favoured by the merchants of the Staple and dealers in wool.[13] In fact, however, this could not have been the case as the Staple was no longer in Westminster in the period 1476–1477.

Caxton's printing press would have resembled in some ways the old cheese press in use at the beginning of the nineteenth century. He would have needed strong, able-bodied apprentices and assistants to carry out what was extremely arduous work. There would have been a storage room with shelves in which were kept holding books or blocks and another room which would have been the casting-house, with a furnace to melt the lead, moulds and matrices for repairing defective type. Without a doubt Wynkyn de Worde was his chief assistant, probably foreman, mechanic and compositor as well in the early days, or until Caxton had been able to train his apprentices. Plomer writes that "Caxton himself no doubt took a large share in the work of printing and correcting in the early days of the press",[14] but this seems highly unlikely. Caxton was really the entrepreneur, the translator, the publisher, if you like, not the actual printer. When things went wrong, or when help was urgently needed, he may have lent a hand, or given advice, but his time would have been fully occupied with translation and preparing and editing material for the press. It is much likelier that he depended to a large extent on his assistant, Wynkyn de Worde. In any event Caxton himself had merely grasped the rudiments of continental printing over a relatively short period and his standards of press work were well below those of Europe. This he knew, but, with his eye on the tremendous possibilities which printing opened up, he was content in the early days to concentrate on small work, preferring to go ahead slowly rather than risk the disasters which had been the fate of some continental printers who had launched their work in too ambitious a fashion.

Robert Copland, reputed to have been the oldest printer in England when he died at a great age in 1548, was originally an apprentice of Caxton. After the latter's death he worked for Wynkyn de Worde and he made it abundantly clear that when Caxton began to print he produced "small storyes and pamflets and so to other".[15] Bishop Moore presented some books to the University of Cambridge which were later examined by the bibliographer, Henry Bradshaw. Among these was one which was thought originally to consist of a single work. Bradshaw's examination revealed that it was made up of eight small stories or pamphlets averaging about twenty quarto leaves each, but without any date. The type was that which is known as Caxton's No. 2 Type, used by Caxton in printing the *Quatre Derrenières Choses*, which he had brought over to England from Bruges.

Caxton's caution—some might call it meanness—in printing was due to a variety of causes—possibly an inferiority complex when he compared himself with the printers of Europe, certainly a fear of overreaching himself financially, a determination to produce works of literature at all costs and to keep down production costs by avoiding the frills and niceties of the trade, while always being confronted with the problem of paper supplies. For example he used no less than 130 different types of paper in one book. This may have been due to the fact that he either had to use up various types of paper, or not print a book at all. It is a problem which has beset many printers, especially those of small local weekly newspapers, even in recent years. Caxton's main aim was to produce books, not to turn out works of art. He only occasionally used head-lines, he eliminated the title page and only had a few wood-cut initial letters and one decorative border. With him it was the reading matter which counted, not how it was presented. He sacrificed appearances for quantity and, in the circumstances, who could say he was wrong. Nobody has ever suggested Caxton was a rich man and he developed his printing on the proverbial shoestring. What Caxton lacked in continental artistry and love of perfectionism he gained in the English genius for improvisation. If he lacked type and there were gaps which had to be filled in, a scribe would write the words into the spaces in the printed text. Space and money were saved by having no punctuation and Caxton's apparent lack of type often caused him to use "i" and "y" indiscriminately and to drop the final "e" in a word. It is notable that he even hyphenated monosyllabic words.

Caxton was a man in a hurry. He was a printer at war, firmly keeping his attention on the main task of propagating the English language in print. His war was against the forces of indolence, reaction, suspicion and indifference, against all who failed to realise that in the whole of Europe there was no language which was so unprogressive or crude as the conglomeration of dialects and primitive phraseology which passed under the euphemism of Middle English.[16]

9

Caxton's Patrons & Friends

JOHN Esteney, the Sacrist of Westminster Abbey, who recorded the renting of a shop to Caxton in 1476, was undoubtedly a useful and powerful ally of the printer, though not a close friend or patron.

Esteney had been made Abbot of Westminster in 1474, a position he held until his death in 1498. Thus he was Abbot throughout the entire period of Caxton's printing in England until the printer's death. He had the task of taking over the guardianship of Elizabeth Woodville, when the Queen and her daughters sought sanctuary at the Abbey for a second time in 1483. It is a measure of the Abbot's power and authority that it was said of him that during the Queen's stay "this church and monastery was enclos'd like a camp, and strictly guarded by soldiers . . . and none were suffer'd to go in and out without special permission, for fear the Princesses should convey themselves over the sea, and baulk Richard III's designs."[1] It is also noteworthy that the obligation for each new Abbot to go to the Vatican to have his appointment confirmed by the Pope was waived in Esteney's time. He was an authoritative, far-sighted Abbot, enthusiastic about his plans for extending the Abbey, ambitious and politically-minded. Caxton would have found it far harder to set up his press if he had not had the Abbot's permission and, presumably, his blessing. For it is unlikely that Caxton would have put on the title pages of some of his early books and words "printed in the Abbey of Westminster" unless the Abbot actually approved and encouraged his work.

It was in his book *The Dictes and Sayings of the Philosophers* that Caxton first recorded in 1477 the actual place of printing and the year of issue of the work. This was the book which was translated by another of Caxton's patrons, the Earl Rivers. On this occasion Caxton merely stated that the book was "emprynted at Westminster". In *The Chronicles of England*, which followed, and in later books, he was more precise: "emprynted by me, Wyllyam Caxton, in thabbey of Westmynstre by

Caxton showing proofs to the Abbot of Westminster. (*Radio Times*)

london, the v day of Juyn, the yere of thincarnacion of our lord god M.CCCC. lxxx." It was this phrase "in the Abbey of Westminster" which caused early biographers to assume that he actually printed inside the precincts of the Abbey.

Esteney was by repute intensely proud of the Abbey and always anxious to draw attention to it, and especially to the building extensions which he personally directed. It may well have been that he was grateful even for such indirect publicity as that which Caxton gave to the Abbey in his books. During the time he was Abbot the nave was completely roofed, the great window set up and much other building work finished.

That Esteney was, contrary to the general indifference of the clergy, keenly interested in Caxton's experiment and may even have taken some credit for it is evident, curiously enough, in one of the few errors of statement made by that normally cautious historian, Stow. The latter, in his *Survey of London*, stated that: "in the Eleemosynary or Almonry at Westminster Abbey, now corruptly called the Ambry, for that the alms of the Abbey were there distributed to the poor, John Islip, Abbot of Westminster, erected the first press of book-printing that ever was in England, and Caxton was the first that practised it in the said Abbey." The reference to John Islip must have been a slip of memory on Stow's part, as this cleric was not Abbot until 1500, but Stow must have had some first-hand information that the Abbot of the day had taken an interest in the printing press and may even have claimed to have sponsored it.

Obviously the precincts of the Abbey would have enabled Caxton to seek advice from learned scribes among the monks on problems of translation from time to time, while the ancient Scriptorium of the Abbey, where books were transcribed, might have been made available to the printer for his researches. That Caxton had at least an acquaintanceship with the Abbot is evident from his own statement in 1490 that: "My Lord Abbot of Westminster did shew to me late certain evidences written in Old English, for to reduce it into our English now used." Yet only a few of Caxton's books were of a distinctly religious character. There was no breviary or book of prayers printed by his press, though there was the *Liber Festivalis*, or *Directions for Keeping the Feasts all the Year*. Many religious publications emanating from Caxton's press might, of course, have been destroyed either before, during or after the Reformation, but it still seems unlikely that there were many of them.

Sir Thomas More put forward an explanation as to why Caxton could not print Bibles even though people would gladly have bought such an edition of Wycliffe's Bible, the first translation into English. Pointing out that Wycliffe's translation was banned by the Church, More wrote: "On account of the penalties ordered by Archbishop Arundel's constitution, though the old translations that were before Wycliffe's day remained lawful and were in some folks' hands had and read, yet he thought no printer would lightly . . . to put any Bible in print at his own charge—and then hang upon a doubtful trial whether the first copy of his translation was made before Wycliffe's days or since. For if it were made since, it must be approved before the printing."

The cautious Caxton would not have taken risks in such an enterprise. Nor would he have chanced incurring the displeasure of the Abbot of Westminster. Apart from which he was a conscientious Catholic.

Yet some of the religious works of Caxton may have vanished altogether, as there is in the Bodleian Library at Oxford a handbill, or advertisement, inviting people to visit his shop to buy a book regulating the Church service.

"If it plese any man spirituel or temporel to bye only Pyes of two and thre comemoracions of Salisburi vse enprynted after the forme of this present lettre whiche ben wel and truly correct, late hym come to Westmonester into the Almonesrye at the reed place and he shal have them good chepe. *Supplico stet cedula.*"*

It is curious that Caxton should make his appeal that the advertisement "should not be pulled down" in Latin. Possibly he felt that Latin carried rather more weight legally with officials who might be tempted to tear down his poster.

A preface to the Liturgy of the Church of England in the early nineteenth century explained what the Pye was and this in its turn provides a clue to one of the many other mysterious words and phrases in the printing trade: "The Number and hardness of the rules called the Pie and the manifold changings of the service, was the cause, that to turn the back only was so hard and intricate a matter, that many

* An actual copy of this advertisement appears on page 118.

Jf it plese ony man spirituel or temporel to bye ony pyes of two and thre comemoracios of salisburi vse enpryntid after the forme of this preset lettre whiche ben wel and truly correct, late hym come to westmonester in to the almonesrye at the reed pale and he shal haue them good chepe .·.·

Suplico stet cedula

Caxton's first "advertisement", indicating that he had set up his printing works at the sign of the Reed (or Red) Pole (Pale), Westminster.

times there was more business to find out what should be read, than to read it when it was found out." The word "pie", of course, has for centuries been used by printers to describe a confused heap of types and it is more than likely that the origin of this phrase lay in the ecclesiastical "Pye".

Far more important than the Abbot of Westminster in the furtherance of Caxton's schemes were his actual patrons. Despite approaches made indirectly, Caxton had failed to obtain the patronage of the Duke of Clarence, which he had tried to get while he was at Bruges. He found his earliest English patrons among the Woodville family, all of whom, including especially Anthony Woodville, the new Earl Rivers, faithfully supported him for many years. It was Rivers who had visited Bruges, where he probably first met Caxton, and who was the printer's first and most enthusiastic patron in England. He was also the most influential patron in these early years as he was a close friend of the King. It may even have been that Earl Rivers gave Caxton some financial backing on his return to London.

That Rivers took an active interest in Caxton's press is obvious from the fact that the printer published the Earl's translation of *The Dictes and Sayings of the Philosophers*, the book which Rivers first read while on his trip to Spain. Caxton's comment on it was:

> "This boke late translate here in sight
> By Antony erle [Rivers] that virtuous knight,
> Please it to accepte to your noble grace,

And at your convenient leisure and space
It to see, reede and understond,
A precious jewell for alle your lond:
For therein is taught, how and in what wise
Men virtues should use and vices despise,
The subjects their princes ever obey,
And they them in right defend ay:—
Thus do every man in his degree
Grant of his grace, the Trinity."

Caxton always waxed eloquently in praise of Rivers, venturing not only into the very rare sly joke as we have seen when he chided the Earl for omitting the passage on women in the translation of *Les Dictes Moraux des Philosophes*, but attempting some ornamental prose of his own. To the last named book Caxton added some verse of his own at the end of the work:

"Go thou little quire, and recommend me
Unto the good grace of my special lord
Th'earl Rivers, for I have emprinted thee
At his commandment, following every word
His copy, as his secretary can record,
At Westminster, of February the XX day,
And of King Edward the xvii day vraye."

Also in the prologue to the book printed from the translation by Earl Rivers of *Cordial*, or *The Four Last Thinges*, Caxton referred to his patron having overcome "great tribulation and adversity", adding that: "it seemeth that he conceiveth well the mutability and the un-stableness of this present life, and that he desireth, with a great zeal and spiritual love, our ghostly help and perpetual salvation." Rivers was then only thirty-six years old. Three years later he was destroyed by the events which followed fast on the death of Edward IV.

It was on 9 April, 1483, that Edward, only forty years old himself, died and the boy King, Edward V, came to the throne. It was natural in the circumstances that Edward IV's brother, Richard Duke of Gloucester, should become Protector. When Edward IV died the new King was in residence at Ludlow with Earl Rivers, his uncle, as his temporary guardian. Richard of Gloucester was visiting the north. The influence of the Woodvilles in royal circles had long been resented by many nobles and gradually there formed against them an alliance of

Richard, Hastings and Buckingham. The Woodvilles controlled the Tower of London and also the fleet of which Sir Edward Woodville was in command. But Richard played a skilled hand in forcing a confrontation. He wrote to the Queen, assuring her of his allegiance to her son, the new King, but gathered together a considerable force to march on London.

At first it seemed as though the whole situation might be decided by a race to the capital by the forces of Rivers and the young King on the one hand and those of Richard on the other. Rivers left the King and his own forces at Stony Stratford and rode back to Northampton where he had learned that Richard had arrived. He greeted Gloucester amicably and that night the two men, together with Buckingham, dined in seemingly cordial fashion. The following morning at dawn Richard had Rivers arrested, after which he rode on to Stony Stratford to meet the King, explaining that he had been bound to make a number of arrests of followers of Edward V because his own life had been threatened. Swiftly and surely Richard seized the real powers of the state and he was confirmed as Protector. Elizabeth Woodville, the widow of Edward IV, was forced to seek sanctuary in Westminster Abbey, while Rivers was beheaded at Pomfret on the instructions of Richard. Shakespeare gives us a portrait of the gallant, intelligent, but unlucky Rivers in his *King Richard III*, act 3, scene 2, where outside Pomfret Castle the guards are conducting Earl Rivers, Lord Grey and Sir Thomas Vaughan to their execution. Rivers comments:

> "Sir Richard Ratcliff, let me tell thee this—
> Today shalt thou behold a subject die,
> For truth, for duty and for loyalty. . . .
> Come, Grey; come, Vaughan, let us Farewell
>   until we meet again in heaven."

Shakespeare may have been indulging in some flights of fancy when he depicted the nobility of this young Earl's demeanour in going so bravely to the scaffold, but he was not apparently far from the truth. A scrap of paper left by Rivers came into the possession of a contemporary historian, John Rouse. John Rouse who lived all his life at Guy's Cliff near Warwick, where he died in 1491, wrote of Rivers: "In the time of his imprisonment at Pomfret he [Rivers] wrote a balet [ballad] in English, which has been shown to me."

Part of this ballad was handed down to Percy, who printed it in his *Reliques*, commenting that: "if we consider that it was written during his cruel confinement in Pomfret Castle, a short time before his execution in 1483, it gives us a fine picture of the composure and steadfastness with which this stout Earl beheld his approaching fate."

Charles Knight—to use his own phrase—reproduced this ballad of Rivers, "modernising the orthography", or at least to some extent:

> "Somewhat musing, and more mourning,
> In remembering the unsteadfastness,
> This world being of such wheeling,
> Me contrarying what may I guess.
> I fear doubtless, remediless
> Is now to seize my woeful chance;
> For unkindness, withouten less
> And no redress, me doth avance,
> With displeasure to my grievance
> And no surance of remedy:
> Lo in this trance, now in substance
> Such is my dance, willing to die.
> Methinks truly bounden am I,
> And that greatly to be content,
> Seeing plainly fortune doth wry
> All contrary from mine intent;
> My life was lent to one intent
> It is nigh spent. Welcome, fortune!
> But I ne went this to be shent,
> But she it meant—such is her wont."[2]

One likes to think that as death approached Rivers hoped that somehow this scrap of paper would be passed on to his friend Caxton who would print it with a prologue of explanation. Alas, this was not to be; nor, one feels, would Caxton have dared publish such a work during the period that led up to Richard's usurpation of the throne, the liquidation of the Woodvilles and their supporters and the murder of the two young princes in the Tower of London.

The death of Edward IV, the disasters which befell the Woodville family and the rise to power of Richard of Gloucester must have posed a threat to Caxton's progress as a printer. Richard did not hesitate to concoct stories of plots and treachery in order to find an excuse for the executions or imprisonment of friends as well as enemies, if this suited his purpose. There was the case of Hastings, Richard's former ally who when accused by the Protector of treason was immediately taken out to be beheaded beside the nearby Chapel. Richard was so anxious to be rid of Hastings that he swore he would not go to dinner until his head was off.

Only the greatest caution could have saved Caxton, a known friend of the Woodvilles, from possible arrest, for printing alone would have seemed sufficiently questionable an enterprise to warrant suspicion in Richard's entourage. Nor could the Church, or even the Abbot easily have saved him. Archbishop Bourchier, a weak Prelate, allowed himself to become the tool of Richard when the Protector requested him to get the young Richard, Duke of York, out of sanctuary. Even the protests of his mother did not stop the Archbishop from agreeing to this plot.

Elizabeth Woodville, Edward IV's Queen and Earl Rivers' sister, was in sanctuary at Westminster Abbey and, as a former patron of Caxton, her close proximity to the printer must have been a matter of some slight embarrassment to him.

A later patron of Caxton was the Lady Margaret Beaufort, who, by her second husband, became Countess of Richmond and Derby, and was the mother of Henry Tudor, the future King Henry VII. The founder of two Cambridge colleges—Christ's and St. John's—Lady Margaret took a keen interest in Caxton's printing press and after Caxton's death supported Wynkyn de Worde. She established many charities and, when she died in 1509, Bishop Fisher said of her in the funeral sermon: "Everyone who knew her loved her, and everything that she said or did became her."

Edward IV had, of course, been a most practical patron. In his reign Caxton had the benefit of the patronage not only of the monarch, but of the Queen, the Duchess Margaret of Burgundy and Earl Rivers. In his prologue and epilogues Caxton stresses again and again that his books had been translated and printed by him "under the shadow of" the King's protection, "or with his protection or suffrance". Edward paid a substantial sum of money in the late 1470's to Caxton for "certain causes or matters performed by him for the said Lord the King".

The sum shown in documents is for £30, which would represent several hundreds of pounds at today's values. This may have been in recognition for what Caxton did for Edward and his supporters when in exile at Bruges, but was almost certainly linked to providing funds for the printing press.

In July, 1482, Caxton published his own version of the translation by Trevisa, chaplain to Lord Berkely, of the *Polychronicon*. This was one of Caxton's first attempts at publishing a major work of such magnitude. He himself not only revised Trevisa's text, but added an historical narrative of his own from the year 1357, when the original text ended, to 1460, when Edward IV came to the throne. The actual work on which Trevisa had based his own version was that of a monk, Ralph Higden, of St. Werburg in Chester, and which some authorities still believe to have been based on an even earlier work. That Caxton was still showing his cautious side even to so friendly a sovereign as Edward IV is plain in the *Proheme* which he added to the book:

"And now at this time simply imprinted and set in forme by me, William Caxton, and a little embellished from the old making, and also have added such stories as I could find from the end that the said Ranulph finished his book, which was the year of our Lord 1357 unto the year of the same 1460, which be a hundred and three years, which work I have finished under the noble protection of my most dread, natural and sovereign lord and most Christian King, King Edward the Fourth, humbly beseeching his most noble grace to pardon me if anything be said therein of ignorance, or otherwise than it ought to be. And also requiring all other to amend whereas there is default, wherein he or they may deserve thank and merit, and I shall pray for them that so do, for I acknowledge my ignorance and simpleness. And if there be thing that may please or profit any man, I am glad that I have achieved it."

Thus Caxton appeared in the role of historian, albeit a diffident one, and he had something to say about this role: "The book is general, touching shortly many notable matters. . . . History is a perpetual observatrice of those things that have been before this present time; and also a quotidian witness of benefits, of malfaits [evil deeds], great acts and triumphal victories of manner of people. And also if the terrible feigned fables of poets have much stirred and moved men to right and conserving of justice, how much more is to be supposed that history, assertrice of virtue and a mother of all philosophy, moving our manners to virtue, reformeth and reconcileth near hand all those men, which through the infirmity of our mortal nature hath led the most part of their life in otiosity, and mis-spended their time, passed right soon out of remembrance: of which life and death is equal oblivion."[3]

In his own historical researches Caxton came up against the problem common to historians of those days—lack of accurate documentary information. He made the point that as few bishops or abbots wrote in their registers there was the risk that many important events went unrecorded. It was to try to fill this gap that Caxton added on his own version of history up to the accession of Edward IV. Here is his own personal description of the marriage of Henry VI to Margaret of Anjou:

". . . king harry married at Southweke queen Margaret. And she came to London the eighteenth day of May [1444]. And by the way all the lords of England received her worshipfully in divers places, and in especial the Duke of Gloucester. And on Blackheath the mayor, alderman and all the crafts in blue gowns embroidered with the device of his craft that they might be beknown, met with her with red hoods, and brought her to London, where were divers pageants and countenances of divers histories showed in divers places of the city, royally and costly. And the thirtyest day of May the said queen was crowned at Westminster. And there was jousts three days during within the sanctuary before the Abbey."[4]

Caxton printed a number of works under the protection and patronage of Edward IV and one assumes he had a measure of patronage from the Earl of Warwick, the Earl of Arundel and later from Richard III. But it would be wrong to regard all these patrons as personal friends or as people deeply involved in his projects. While there were a few special patrons who were both friends and practically interested in his work, such as Margaret of Burgundy and Earl Rivers, there were other "patrons" who, like the Duke of Clarence, neither knew him nor cared about him. Patronage in the fifteenth century was not as a rule like that of the eighteenth when patrons were the close friends of artists and poets. Patronage in Caxton's time was more a question of the artist or innovator seeking to win tacit support by flattery than anything else. The dedication of a book did not mean that the printer had been paid by the person dedicated. It is true that Caxton speaks sometimes of "great rewards" to him and that such phrases have been interpreted

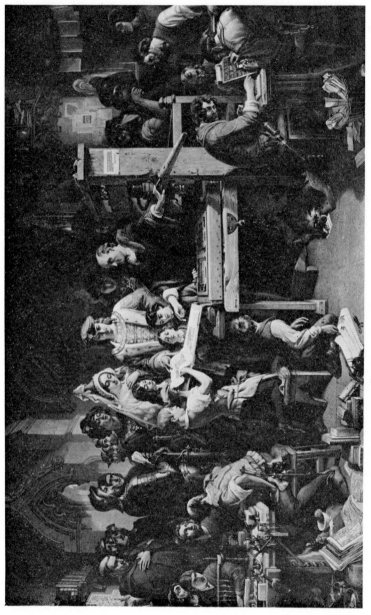

Caxton showing proofs to Edward IV at Westminster, from a 19th-century painting by Maclise. (*Radio Times*)

as meaning that he was handsomely paid for his book projects. This was rarely the case: the talk of "great rewards" meant little more than that the "patron" so referred to had nodded approval, or offered to accept the presentation of a book. As Plomer says: "Like the ruff and the farthingale, such language was the fashion of the time."[5]

Plomer adds that Caxton's customers, "peer and commoner alike, paid him for his work as a printer, but he was under no sort of obligation to them, and Caxton was just the man to print a good book, even if he lost by it, rather than his countrymen should want it. His judgement in the choice of books was sound. Before the end of 1478 twenty-one books can be traced to his press."[6]

It is, however, unlikely that Caxton would have risked his own money in printing any book which he did not think would sell. He did not lose money by his printing: had he done so, he would never have produced so much or for so long a period. One must remember that only for a relatively short time did he hold the record of being England's first printer. Within two years of his arrival in Westminster there was the report of the still unknown printer at Oxford and a year later one hears of the "schoolmaster printer of St. Albans", while in 1480 a Lithuanian printer named John Lettou came to London and set up a press actually inside the City, issuing a book in folio called *Antonius Andreae, Questiones super XII, libros metaphysicae.*

John Lettou had learned the craft of printing more thoroughly and under better teachers than had Caxton. He also had the advantage of a base inside the privileged and highly restrictive City of London. It is curious that Lettou did not come to London under the auspices of the Stationer's Guild, but of that of a Mercer named William Wilcock.

Though Lettou may have been technically a better printer, though both the unknown printer of Oxford (said to have been Theodoric Rood) and the "schoolmaster of St. Albans" were practising their craft for about seven years, not one of these three offered any real competition to Caxton. Lettou finally went into partnership with another printer. Not one of them equalled Caxton's feats of production, and the reason for their failures is not hard to find: they did not print in the English language. In this field Caxton was not only first, but supreme.

Bishop Bale, in the first edition of his history of English literature published in 1548, said that Caxton was first prompted to tackle the translation of the *Polychronicon*: "by the unfinished attempts of a certain schoolmaster or literary preceptor at the shrine of St. Albans. This man had been prevented by death from completing his work, though the individual pages had been laid out in order. Caxton not only assembled them, but also made several additions."[7]

This raises the question of Caxton's relationship with his rivals. Plomer writes that: "the competition of these various rivals woke Caxton up to the necessity of showing more interest in the mechanical side of his art. Accordingly between the years 1478 and 1481 he effected certain changes for the better. The type that he had been using ever since his settlement at Westminster was getting worn, so he trimmed it and recast some of the letters."[8] Yet it does not seem that Caxton worried himself in the least about his competitors. He knew that he was ploughing an altogether different field and one which promised a richer yield. As to the schoolmaster at St. Albans, Caxton was probably on the best of terms with him in the light of Bishop Bale's disclosures. But it seems probable, as has been pointed out by Dr. Scott, the former Keeper of the Muniments of Westminster Abbey, that this schoolmaster printer did not operate at St. Albans in Hertfordshire, but in a house known as St. Albans in the precincts of Westminster Abbey and close to Caxton's own shop. Dr. Scott referred to a certain Otwel Fulle or Fuller, who was master of the scholars of the Almonry at Westminster.[9]

If this was indeed the case, then it is not unlikely that Caxton and Otwel Fulle were friends, exchanging opinions on printing and the techniques involved and perhaps Otwel Fulle did urge Caxton to carry on his work, should he die. Otwel is known to have used a fount of type similar to that of Caxton.

Conceivably, the secret of much of Caxton's success was that his quiet, unostentatious demeanour, his sagacity and humility made him acceptable to many, while unacceptable to none. If not a monk, he was essentially a man of the cloisters, immersed in his work and never one to get himself involved in unnecessary arguments or political plotting. He had a wide range of friends and acquaintances, to whom he often referred in his works. There was, for example, William Daubney, Treasurer to King Henry VI, described by Caxton as his "good and singular friend".[10] He had a long association with the Earl of Warwick, dating back to Caxton's term of office as Governor of the English Nation. Richard Whitehill, Lieutenant of Guines, who was appointed by the King with Caxton to negotiate the renewal of the trade treaty with Burgundy in 1464, was a servant of the Earl of Warwick. But this association with Warwick was almost certainly an embarrassment to Caxton later when Warwick led the rebellion of 1470–1: the pardon which the printer obtained in Cologne in the early seventies "to cover all offences" was almost certainly meant to exonerate him from accusations of being involved in Warwick's revolt just as the dedication of his *Chess Book* to the Duke of Clarence was intended to acknowledge the latter being received back into favour.

Then again Sir John Fastolf, an avid book collector, was another patron to whom Caxton dedicated his volume of 1481, which contained *Of Old Age*, *Of Friendship* and *Declamation of Noblesse* and in addition a tribute to Sir John. It is possible, but by no means certain, that Sir John contributed towards the cost of this work, as, though the actual translator has never been discovered, Caxton wrote that the book was published after much labour and cost and copies of the original manuscript from which the translation was made were obviously scarce as he said that he had only been able to obtain a copy with great difficulty and at some considerable expense. If Sir John did not contribute towards the cost of this enterprise, one must assume that Caxton's sound judgement as an editor was once more justified. He might well have been writing for that always rising but ever ageing society of today—the rapidly increasing army of the retired. For, in his preface he said he had printed it so that "noble virtuous and well-disposed men who were getting on in years" might find some advice and consolation in it. Few copies of the original work were available and Caxton in this instance knew his market as surely as those who in recent years have founded *Pre-Retirement Choice* for those about to retire or who have actually retired.

Henry Plomer has stated that: "the Earl of Worcester not only welcomed the advent of Caxton's press, but brought him books . . . to print."[11] This could not have been the case, as the Earl of Worcester was executed in the sudden upsurge in the fortunes of the House of Lancaster in 1470–1471, some five years before Caxton started to print in England. It is doubtful whether Caxton ever met Worcester, even though he printed two of the Earl's translations (*Declamation of Noblesse* was one) long after the latter's death. The truth is that the Earl of Worcester was the umpire in that celebrated tournament between

Anthony Woodville and the Bastard of Burgundy in 1467, and probably Worcester was a friend of Woodville. If one reads what Caxton has to say about Worcester, it is clear that the Earl was a man who complied with Caxton's always stringent views on how a noble should comport himself. Among the nobility, wrote Caxton, "none was his peer" and the Earl "excelled in virtue and cunning" [knowledge]. He had "visited the holy places of Jerusalem . . . and the Pope". Yet Caxton does not pay tribute to what was perhaps the finest of Worcester's qualities— his stalwart efforts to encourage in England a revival of classical scholar- ship to match that of Italian humanism. By instinct, as a merchant and a self-made philosopher and thinker, Caxton realised the Earl had such virtues, but as one who could not claim to be a scholar and was inhibited in expressing himself freely on such matters, he failed to spell this out, because the academic theories surrounding the New Learning were somewhat of a mystery to him. This is not to make a quibble or in any way to denigrate Caxton, or his lack of scholarship, but more to show that his instincts were sound and that he lamented his death and recog- nised him as a great soldier, statesman and bibliophil.

When Edward IV died and Richard of Gloucester became Protector, Caxton was in the midst of producing his edition of the *Golden Legend*. It was a large and expensive project and Caxton was forced to pause before going ahead. If he delayed publication, the money he had already spent on the project could well be lost. But in the political crisis of the period it was not easy to find a guarantee of support. Eventually Caxton obtained the backing of the Earl of Arundel. It is said that the Earl called in on Caxton one day at the Red Pale offices and was told that the printer proposed to cease work on the *Golden Legend*. It was then that Arundel encouraged him to go ahead, agreeing to buy a number of copies when it was printed and made his offer of "the gift of a buck in summer and a doe in winter".

Yet on this occasion Caxton seems to have turned to the Church as a valuable neutral ally in times of political crisis. For he gave fifteen copies of the *Golden Legend* to St. Margaret's Church. By 1500 fourteen of these had been sold at prices ranging from 6s. 8d. to 5s. 4d. Possibly Caxton made several gifts of books to the Abbey to retain the approval of the authorities, as in 1520 the Keeper of St. Edmund's Shrine still had "a paper masseboke of Salisburi's use of William Caxton's gyfte".

Such help was doubtless all important, but even more crucial was the backing of a peer who was close to the entourage of Richard III and had just been appointed Master of the Game of the royal forests. That Caxton had to trim his sails to take advantage of the changes in the monarchy and in the government is certain. Either he did so and continued with his printing, or he ceased to be a printer and disappeared into the anonymity of an ageing merchant. Quite rightly Caxton came down in favour of continuing with his press, but this is not to say that he did not remain discreetly loyal to old friends and patrons. For example, there was his work, *Knight of the Tower*, already mentioned, which he said had been requested by "a noble lady" with daughters. This book was published in 1483 when Edward IV's widowed Queen, Elizabeth Woodville, was in sanctuary at Westminster. Probably this work was commissioned some years before and, while Caxton did not go so far as to name a Queen who was out of favour at the Court, he made indirect acknowledgement to her. Even this gesture may have been a risky one.

Then again in 1484, the first year of the reign of Richard III, Caxton published *The Subtil Histories and Fables of Aesop*, translated from the French. Now in this book Caxton introduced a rare feature in his works and, in doing so, laid himself open to a charge of deliberately and maliciously insulting the King. It was only very occasionally that Caxton used wood-prints in his books and these were imported from overseas. But in the first leaf of this book there is a portrait of Aesop, a large, somewhat crude woodcut depicting him as having a large head, long jaws, sharp eyes and a curved back. Whether or not Richard III was deformed with a hunchback, as Shakespeare alleged, the description of Aesop to some extent fitted that of the King. If Richard was a hunchback, then Caxton was taking an enormous risk in allowing the book to be published. The question which is difficult to answer is whether he realised what he was doing; if, indeed, this was not a subtle sign to his erstwhile supporters, such as the Queen Elizabeth herself, that secretly Caxton was on their side.

From all we know of Caxton he would have taken no such risk, had he thought there was the slightest chance of such a snide satire being spotted by the King or any of his courtiers. But one cannot be sure that he would not have calculated the risks very carefully and felt confident that his subtlety would be lost on the Court, if not on the lady in sanctuary.

King Richard III: lukewarm patron of Caxton. (*Radio Times*)

It was in this book about Aesop in which Caxton added on at the end of the Fables a story of his own, one which might well have had a message for some opponents of the King. It is as follows:

". . . I will finish all these fables with this tale that followeth, which a worshipful priest and a parson told me late: he said that there were dwelling at Oxenford two priests, both Masters of Arts—of whom that one was quick and could put himself forth; and that other was a good simple priest. And so it happened, that the master that was pert and quick was anon promoted to a benefice or twain, and after to pre-bends, and for to be a dean of a great prince's chapel, supposing and weening that his fellow, the simple priest, should never be promoted, but be always an annual, or at the most, a parish priest.

"So, after a long time that this worshipful man, this dean, came running into a good parish with five or seven horses, like a prelate, and came into the church of the said parish, and found there this good simple man, sometime his fellow, which came and welcomed him lowly. And that other bade him 'Good morrow, Master John', and took him slightly by the hand, and asked him where he dwelt, and the good man said, 'In this parish.'

" 'How,' said he, 'are ye here a sole priest, or a parish priest?'

" 'Nay, sir,' said he, 'for lack of a better, though I be not able nor worthy, I am parson and curate of this parish.'

"And then that other lowered his bonnet and said, 'Master Parson, I pray you to be not displeased; I had supposed ye had not been beneficed. But master,' said he, 'I pray you what is this benefice worth to you a year?'

" 'Forsooth,' said the good simple man, 'I wot never; for I make never accounts thereof, how well I have had it four or five years.'

" 'And know ye not,' said he, 'what it is worth? It should be a good benefice.'

" 'No, forsooth,' said he, 'but I wot well what it shall be worth to me.'

" 'Why,' said he, 'what shall it be worth?'

" 'Forsooth,' said he, 'if I do my true dealing in the cure of my parishes in preaching and teaching, and do my part belonging to the cure, I shall have heaven therefore. And if their souls be lost, or any of them, by my default, I shall be punished therefore. And hereof I am sure.'

"And with that word the rich dean was abashed, and thought he should be the better, and take more heed to his cures and benefices than he had done. This was a good answer of a good priest and an honest man. And herewith I finish this book, translated and imprinted by me, William Caxton."

The printer may have got away with a few sly asides in his works, but as an editor and publisher with a keen political sense he was swift to smell danger and to take steps to avoid it. When he brought out a new edition of the *Game of Chess* in 1483 he made a point of omitting the name of the Duke of Clarence to whom the book had originally been dedicated. The Duke had been executed in the meantime. Similarly he was cautious in his references to the Woodville family name after the accession of Richard III and the execution of Earl Rivers. *The Curial*, which Caxton translated from the French and issued on 13 June, 1483, was almost certainly intended originally to be dedicated to Earl Rivers: instead Caxton merely offered it "for a noble and virtuous Earl". But when the printer produced his third edition of *The Dictes and Sayings of the Philosophers* in 1489, Earl Rivers' name was kept in exactly as it had been in the first edition. By this time Richard III had been killed on Bosworth Field, and Henry VII had not only come to the throne, but married yet another Elizabeth Woodville, the daughter of Edward IV and Queen Elizabeth.

This is not to suggest that Caxton was a Vicar of Bray in his trade. He had to be circumspect, as much to guard his secret patrons and supporters as for himself, and, if one considers all the evidence, especially the dedications to anonymous persons during Richard III's reign, there is little doubt where his sympathies lay. It is also extremely doubtful whether Richard III took much interest, if any at all, in printing, as only one book was dedicated to him.

Possibly Caxton was working under greater difficulties than mere evidence can suggest. There is no indication that the Court of Richard III in any way accepted him, and he may even have been suspected by some of them of being an agent of the opposition to Richard's rule. The Earl of Arundel, after permitting a dedication to him and offering some help, seems to have cooled off, as only one book was dedicated to him. After this Caxton did a curious thing, one that can perhaps be interpreted as a desperate bid for recognition in official circles. When, on 23 December, 1483, he completed his translation of *Caton*, he made the dedication not to any friend or patron, but to the City of London. It might be argued that this was a friendly and even sentimental gesture to the city where he had served his apprenticeship and with which, through the Mercers' Company, he had been so closely associated for so many years.

Perhaps on this occasion Caxton obtained some financial backing from merchants in the City, but, if so, there is no evidence of it. N. F. Blake writes that the work itself may have inclined Caxton to make this dedication, "for in his prologue he compares the customs of Rome with those of London. The book was designed to improve the morals of merchants rather than to amuse the nobility."[12]

This theory is, of course, a reasonable possibility, but from what we know of Caxton he never acted on mere whims: in all his work, translating, editing and printing there is the pattern of a man who moved forward by a series of impulses and logical steps rather than on one single motive. This was not the behaviour of a devious man, but of one whose logic was based on commonsense rather than academic theory. When Caxton decided to print a book he had not one reason, but several. In the world of literature and publishing he adopted the policy of military planners: he believed in defence in depth. In the publication of *Caton* (Cato on morals) one can only guess at this logical progress. In the first instance Caxton realised there was a useful and apt comparison between Rome and London. Argument number one for involving the City of London. He was short of patrons and he needed desperately to establish himself as a patriotic subject with loyalty to the one institution which every King in this age needed—the support of the City of London. This could have been a useful political ploy.

Probably because of his political astuteness he was able even in the difficult times of Richard III's reign to carry on turning out books. This astuteness was retained when Richard was killed and Henry VII succeeded, for in December, 1485, when *Charles the Great* was printed, Caxton stated that the book had been requested by William Daubney, but showed great tact in referring to him as "Treasurer of the Jewels of Edward IV", and making no reference to the offices he held under Richard III. The probability is that Daubney was one of the people instrumental in obtaining manuscripts and books for Caxton so that he could select material to translate and print, as he was a Searcher of the Port at the Port of London both under Edward IV and Richard III.

One of his greatest friends was William Pratt, or Praat, who was born in Canterbury and may possibly have known Caxton when he was a lad in the Weald of Kent. This was the William Pratt who was fined along with Caxton in 1453 for failing to attend the election of the Lord Mayor of London. He lent Caxton one of his books to be translated and printed—the *Book of Good Manners*, published in 1487, though it must have been planned and commissioned much earlier, probably about 1484. Pratt died in July, 1486 and there is no mention in his will either of Caxton or of the book. Pratt was the only member of the Mercers' Company to be mentioned in any of Caxton's prologues or epilogues. It is possible that Caxton was at this time toying with the idea of printing books which had greater appeal for the merchant class than for the aristocracy. If so, it was a measure of his failure to obtain support from patrons in Court circles, but in books published at this time there would seem to be less of the purely romantic works and much more of the practical. The *Book of Good Manners* could be said to apply to the bourgeois merchants just as much as *Caton*, with its comparisons with Rome, could be of more interest to the City of London than to the Court. *The Royal Book* or *Book for a King* was actually ordered either by the Mercers' Company or by an individual Mercer, possibly Pratt himself, in this same period. Its dedication stated that the book was "compiled and made at the request of King Philip of France . . . and translated to English by me, William Caxton, at the request of a worshipful merchant and Mercer of London."

Many copies of this book still exist, which is some evidence of its popularity. The title *The Royal Book* may have been another example of Caxton's discreet editing with an eye to securing favour at the Court. It was not the title by which the book was best known by merchants and others in the City of London, which may reveal how unpopular Richard III really was. The common title given to this work was *The Book of Vices and Virtues*.

Linguist and Editor

ESPITE what the critics may say about Caxton's lack of scholarship and academic training, it is as a linguist and editor that he deserves to take his place in history rather than as printer or publisher.

A century before John de Trevisa had pointed to the difficulty which the English had in understanding one another, how a man, in say London, could not grasp what a man from nearby Kent was talking about, "For jangle that one never so fast that other is never the wiser", was Trevisa's comment on how a man from one part of the country baffled one from another area. Chaucer said much the same thing when he referred to the "so great diversity in English and in writing of our tongue", and all this was still true in Caxton's time.

Caxton himself appears to have been in a curious dilemma in his approach to this problem of the still developing, and in many respects immature English tongue. That he desperately wanted to recreate the works of Latin and French writers in the English language is undoubted. He could probably have succeeded much more easily as a printer if he had merely copied Latin and French works, relying on a continental as well as a limited English market. But he chose deliberately to return to London to print in his mother tongue.

We have already noted his early struggles with translations, the rebuke and encouragement of the Duchess Margaret of Burgundy, his own dissatisfaction with his progress. But, as book succeeded book, Caxton became more confident, and that confidence showed most in what he increasingly interpolated into his translations, and the comments in his preface and epilogues. In these things Caxton revealed the true man, though even so he kept sufficiently tight a rein on his thoughts to permit us little more than a peep into his mind.

His "Frenchified English" has already been noted. It was partly a fondness for the ornateness of French and a feeling that French words had more universality of expression than had many English words. But it was originally no doubt an attempt to keep conscientiously to the original meaning, using French literary constructions in his translations—or, as he put it: "after my simple and poor cunning . . . as nigh as I can or may." Often he mixed direct and indirect speech and some passages of Caxton could be described as "Pidgin French" or "Pidgin English", much like what one finds among the native populations of the Pacific Ocean today. But Caxton introduced many new words into the English language, many of which are current today, and his adaptations of French words were sufficiently apt to become popular. In this respect he played a remarkable role in strengthening and enriching the English language.

It could be argued by purists that any educated Englishman who had spent thirty years on the continent could not fail to improve and add to the English language, especially as French had become the accepted tongue of the cultured. This is perfectly true, but the reason why Caxton made such an impact was that he spread his version of the English language by printing it.

He admired Chaucer's pithiness and descriptive powers, but he followed the contemporary fondness for "curious gaye terms" and "the new eloquence". Curt Buhler makes the point that Caxton "emphasised and promoted" rather than initiated the taste for translations from French.[1] He was fully conscious of the fact that he had an uphill task in that the new learning had not seriously touched England as yet. Many have criticised Caxton for printing translations of second and third-rate literature rather than major classical works. It is doubtful whether he could have made adequate translations of the best of the classics, or if they would have been appreciated in English. The foundations of English scholarship were really only being founded in Henry VI's reign: it was another half century before many great scholars were produced. What Caxton chose to print was not merely what certain courtiers and nobles wanted to read, but what they could easily understand. Herein lay his talent both as a modest translator and an astute editor.

Some quotations from Caxton's prologue to *Eneydos* have already been utilised in this narrative. But in assessing Caxton as both translator and editor, it is necessary to look again at what he had to say here, because this contains much of the key to his methods and views. There is his thoroughness: "I . . . forthwith took a pen and ink and wrote a leaf or twain, which I oversaw again to correct it." Then again we have a picture of Caxton summing up the problems posed by his critics: "And when I saw the fair and strange terms therein, I doubted that it should not please some gentlemen which late blamed me, saying that in my translations I had over-curious terms which could not be understood of common people and desired me to use old and homely terms in my translations. And fain would I satisfy every man, and so to do took an old book and read therein, and certainly the English was so rude and broad that I could not well understand it. And also my Lord Abbot of Westminster did show to me late certain evidences written in old English for to reduce it into our English now used, and certainly it was written in such wise that it was more like Dutch than English. I could not reduce, nor bring it to be understood, and certainly our language now used varyeth far from that which was used and spoken when I was born . . . and that common English that is spoken in one shire varyeth from another."[2]

Here is some proof of how the English language had visibly changed in Caxton's own lifetime, as, of course, it has in most men's lifetime, but in the fifteenth century those changes were swifter and more dynamic. They must also have been perplexing to many and it was this very perplexity which Caxton understood and defined when he wrote: "For in these days every man that is in any reputation in his country will utter his communication and matters in such manners and terms that few men shall understand them. And some honest and great clerks have been with me and desired me to write the most curious terms that I could find. And thus between plain rude and curious, I stand abashed. But in my judgement the comma terms that be daily used be lighter to be understood than the old and ancient English. And forasmuch as this present book is not for a rude, uplandish man to labour therein, nor read it, but only for a clerk and a noble gentleman . . . therefore, as a man between both, I have reduced and translated this said book into our English not over-rude nor curious, but in such terms as shall be understood, by God's grace, according to my copy. And if any man will occupy himself in reading of it and findeth such terms that he cannot understand, let him go read and learn Virgil, or the Epistles of Ovid, and there he shall see and understand lightly all, if he have a good reader and informer. For this book is not for every rude and uncunning man to see, but to clerks and to very gentlemen that understand gentlemen and science. Then I pray all them that shall read in this little treatise to hold me and excuse me for translating it, for I acknowledge myself ignorant of cunning to emprise on me so high and noble a work."3

Caxton had the advantage of knowing and appreciating such works in English as those of Chaucer and Lydgate as well as being competent in and delighting in "the fair language of French". But he had an unfortunate habit of starting off a thesis of his own concoction simply and intelligently and then, possibly through tiredness or lack of vocabulary, tailing off into a style which was diffuse and lacking in clarity. Caxton is often paradoxically enough least clear when he is impressing the need for clarity, as the latter part of the quotation in the last paragraph shows. But as Caxton printed books so his critical faculties were stimulated and so he began to grasp that a dialogue between readers and printer, or readers and editor and translator, was essential. Criticisms of his work may have been relatively few and possibly few of them actually reached him, but his later publications suggest that he did take them seriously and even acted on some of them. When he started to print the works of Chaucer, he was well aware of all the difficulties the task presented as well as the critical opinions of others of Chaucer's now somewhat archaic vocabulary and phraseology. He had just as much a job of translation to do as if he were working on a French script.

Dr. Dibdin, in his *Typographical Antiquities*, referring to Caxton, said: "Our typographer contrived, though well stricken in years, to translate not fewer than five thousand closely printed folio pages. As a translator, therefore, he ranks among the most laborious, and, I would hope, not the least successful of his tribe. The foregoing conclusion is the result of a careful enumeration of all his books translated as well as printed by him; which [the translated books], if published in modern fashion, would extend to twenty-five octavo volumes!"4

Caxton writing on Chaucer is of special interest, as he reveals Caxton the literary critic as well as the translator and editor. In his preface to the second edition of the *Canterbury Tales*, possibly after some criticisms had reached his ears, he said, "we ought to give a singular laud unto that noble and great philosopher, Geoffrey Chaucer, the which for his ornate writing in our tongue, may well have the name of a laureate poet. For before that he, by his labour, embellished, ornated and made fair our English tongue, in this royaume . . . he made many books and treatises of many a noble history, as well in metre as in rhyme and prose; and them so craftily made, that he comprehendeth his matters in short, quick and high sentences; eschewing prolixity, casting away the chaff of superfluity, and showing the picked grain of sentence, uttered by crafty and sugared eloquence." On another occasion he refers to Chaucer as excelling "in my opinion all other writers in our English, for he writeth no void words, but all his matter is full of high and quick sentence . . . For of him all other have borrowed sith and taken in all their well saying and writing."

But Caxton, in printing Chaucer, was also up against the problem that the manuscripts of the great writer were in private hands and varied considerably in their texts, as books must have done when they were produced by different transcribers. Referring to this, Caxton wrote that "of which book so incorrect was one brought to me six year passed, which I had supposed had been very true and correct, and according to the same I did imprint a certain number of them, which anon were sold to many and divers gentlemen: of whom one gentleman came to me and said that this book was not according in many places unto the book that Geoffrey Chaucer had made. To whom I answered that I had made it according to my copy, and by me was nothing added or diminished. Then he said he knew a book which his father had and much loved, that was very true, and according unto his own first book by him made; and said more, if I would imprint it again, he would get me the same book for a copy. How be it, he wist well his father would not gladly part from it; to whom I said, in case that he could get me such a book true and correct, that I would once endeavour me to print it again, for to satisfy the author: whereas before by ignorance I erred in hurting and defaming his book in divers places, in setting in some things that he had never said nor made, and leaving out many things that he made which are requisite to be set in it. And thus we fell at accord; and he full gently got me of his father the said book, and delivered it to me, by which I have corrected my book."

Such was Caxton's admiration for Chaucer and his great concern to get things right that, prudent and cautious as he was in his general attitude to printing, he put accuracy above all else and always paid careful heed to the criticisms and comments of his customers. Perhaps he was concerned as much for his own reputation and what his customers thought of him as for scrupulous accuracy, but this in itself was no bad quality in a printer and publisher.

Caxton was not above taking short cuts and even making drastic paraphrases in some of his works, both in English and in translations, but such was his admiration for Chaucer that he took greater pains to be accurate in printing such books as *Boethius* and *The Canterbury Tales*. His prologues and epilogues reveal how deeply concerned he was that his Chaucerian work should be clear to all readers and he invited "correction and amendment". But this is not to say that Caxton the editor did not have to intervene on occasions and take agonising decisions as how best to present a Chaucerian manuscript. William Blades mentions the problem Caxton had in printing Chaucer's *Book of Fame*: "Manuscripts of this poem were, probably, even in our printer's time, difficult to obtain. The copy used by him was certainly very imperfect. Many lines are altogether omitted, and in the last page Caxton was evidently in a great strait, for his copy was deficient 66 lines, probably occupying one leaf in the original. We know from his own writings the great reverence in which our printer held the 'noble poet', and we can imagine his consternation when the choice had to be made, either to follow his copy and print nonsense, from the break of ideas caused by the deficient verses, or to step into Chaucer's shoes and supply the missing links from his own brain."[5]

Like all good editors Caxton adopted the bold course, that of supplying the missing links himself. Even so he acted cautiously, supplying not 66 lines out of his own head, but writing in a simple link of a mere two lines of his own composition.

The actual version ran like this, Caxton's two lines being shown in italics:

> "They were a chekked bothe two
> And neyther of hym might out goo
> *And wyth the noyse of themwo*
> *I suddenly awoke anon tho*
> And remembryd what I had seen
> And how hye and ferre I had been."[6]

In the best tradition of modern scholars Caxton put his name in the margin of the page against the two lines he had composed, but he gave no explanation of what he had done.

With other works Caxton frequently showed his authority as an editor and made alterations of his own in scripts. It is not always possible to decide exactly where he made such alterations as frequently the only surviving text of such a work is Caxton's own. He did not, as far as can be seen, interfere with any works of his patrons, but he altered *Morte Darthur* quite considerably and Trevisa's translation of the monk, Ralph Higden. Caxton was obviously highly critical of Malory and made many cuts and changes in his printed version. Malory made great play of alliteration in his text of *Morte Darthur* and Caxton took pains to tone this down. For example Malory's phrase "up to the crest of the crag" became in Caxton's version "ascended up to that hill" and "a werlow woll" became "a devil".

Where necessary, too, Caxton would modernise a text: he did this with much of Trevisa's work. But here he took a line quite different from his ruthless re-writing of Malory. Trevisa also indulged in alliteration, but not in the same crude and unmusical doggerel style of Malory. Thus Caxton printed Trevisa's alliterative phrases. On the other hand he regarded some of Trevisa's writing as old fashioned and needing to be "a little embellished".

But Edward Gibbon, the historian who regarded history as little more than a register of the crimes, follies and misfortunes of mankind, made a harsh judgment on Caxton. "In the choice of his authors, that liberal and industrious artist was reduced to comply with the vicious taste of his readers; to gratify the nobles with treatises on heraldry, hawking and the game of chess, and to amuse the popular credulity with romances of fabulous knights and legends of more fabulous saints." It is a rather biased and sweeping condemnation, but even Gibbon could not avoid paying tribute to Caxton's attempts to set on record some of the history of England. But Gibbon surprisingly missed the vital point that Caxton was not only modestly helping to record history on his own account, but was actually making history by printing in English. Or, as Thomas Warton, the eighteenth century author of *The History of English Poetry*, put it: "It was a circumstance favourable at least to English literature, owing indeed to the general illiteracy of the times that our first printers were so little employed on books written in the learned languages. Almost all Caxton's books are English. The multiplication of English copies multiplied English readers, and these again produced new vernacular writers. The existence of a press induced many persons to turn authors, who were only qualified to write in their natives tongue."

As a translator Caxton limited his work mainly to handling books and manuscripts in French, in which language he was proficient. But he almost certainly spoke Flemish and Dutch equally well and, as Governor of the English Nation in Bruges, he would need to have a knowledge of Latin. In *The Life of Saynt Rockes*, which is part of the *Golden Legend* he stated that it was "translated out of Latin by me, William Caxton". He is also believed to have translated from the Latin *The Declamation of Noblesse*.

That he must have been a fairly speedy translator is obvious from his output. True, there are signs that in the early days, when he was not so sure of himself, he took a long time over a single translation and frequently worked over and over again on the same passage until he got it right. Later he seems on occasions to have rushed his translation and to have skipped whole passages, though this was by no means a frequent occurrence. During the seventeen years that he printed books he translated between twenty and thirty and it is even possible that he translated others which never reached his press. It is impossible to assess his speed, but we do know that it took him ten weeks to translate *The Mirror of the World*. This may have been due to pressure from his patron, Alderman Hugh Brice of the City of London, who wanted the book printed so that he could present it to Lord Hastings. Brice must have been one of Caxton's sterner taskmasters for this book is illustrated by wood engravings, which the printer normally did not use.

Caxton took rather longer with other translations; eight months over *The Knight of the Tower*, which was only ten pages longer than *The Mirror of the World*, and as long as eleven months over *Good Manners*, which was a mere 132 pages.

It has already been noted that there was no demand for Bibles in the vernacular in the fifteenth century and that there were serious obstacles to attempting to print them. Caxton made it quite clear in his prologue to *Charles the Great* that he earned his living by printing, implying that he needed to make a profit. Had he gone to the expense of printing a Bible in the vernacular and then seen it banned from sale by the ecclesiastical authorities, such a blow could well have finished his career as a printer. No doubt the main reason was that there was no demand for Bibles and therefore no money to be made from printing them. But Caxton, being a devout Christian, contrived to work a number of biblical stories into his works. The *Golden Legend* includes a number of these such as the narrative of Adam and Eve, the stories of Job and of Saul and David. Some of the narrative appears to follow the Bible very closely, but Caxton broke off to insert this comment of his own: "And here I leave all the story and make an end of the *Book of Kings* for this time. For yet that wish to know how every king reigned after that, ye may find it in the first chapter of St. Matthew, which is read on Christmas morning."

Dr. Pierce Butler, of the John Hopkins University in Baltimore, made a study, published in 1899, of the *Golden Legend*, indicating how Caxton had added Biblical stories to the legends of the saints. "This portion of Caxton's *Golden Legend* is little more than a disguised version of the Bible," he wrote. "He dared not publish the Bible as such, for that would smell of Wycliff and rank Lollardy, and Caxton had no ambition to stir up the powers that were in Church or State, but he evaded the vigilance of the laws by inserting Bible stories in his *Golden Legend*", which became "one of the principal instruments in preparing the way for the Reformation."[7]

This last assertion is somewhat sweeping and wide of the mark. The introduction of printing may have been one of the lesser factors in preparing the way for the Reformation in England, but it should be remembered that in this country it began with a revolution in the constitution of the Church without any change of doctrine and in many respects retained a more continuous connection with the old Church than would have been permitted by the leading continental Church reformers. Almost anything Caxton did or printed would tend towards the maintenance of such a continuous link rather than a break with it.

N. F. Blake makes one of the most sensible comments when he writes that: "Caxton is important because he is one of the few people who discuss what they are trying to do. Too many other fifteenth century authors have merely left translations without giving us any insight into their method of working."[8] Or, put it another way, while Caxton has provided us with disappointingly few clues about his life, he has provided us with an abundantly clear portrait of his work as translator, author, critic, editor, publisher and printer. It is all there in the prologues and epilogues and in those occasional interpolations of his own work which he puts into the works of others.

His faults as a translator, editor and publisher were more or less typical of his time. Much has been made by some critics of his "exaggerated lip service to royalty and the nobility". But Caxton was only following the custom of his time and in any event, as a sound business man, was merely trying to win clients by flattery. Sometimes he repeated himself unnecessarily, but this may have been due partly to hurried translation and editing. As we have seen some works were rushed through at high speed, whereas others were taken more leisurely.

He has also been criticised for not seriously developing his printing to come up to continental standards, but this is rather churlish in the circumstances. Many continental printers spent considerable sums in improving their technique only to find they could no longer carry on. Caxton maintained his press for the best part of twenty years and was able to hand it on to Wynkyn de Worde to preserve for posterity. Though he rarely employed wood-cuts, he was sufficiently good an editor to realise that his *Game and Play of Chess* required illustrations and these he provided with woodcuts in the second edition. Blades remarked that the woodcuts in this volume numbered only sixteen, not twenty-four as "Dibdin and other writers say, eight of them being impressions from blocks used for previous chapters."

This edition of *Game and Play of Chess* was the first book in the English language which contained woodcuts on this scale. They were extremely crude illustrations, but they served their purpose in depicting the game of chess. A figure is shown sitting at a table with a chessboard before him and holding one of the chess-men in his hand. In another woodcut a king and another person are seen playing chess, while in a third a king, seated on his throne, is bent over the game. All the pieces of the chess-board are depicted in some way or other; the king and queen; the *alphyns*, now called "bishops", depicted as "in the manner of judges, sitting"; the knight; the rook, or castle, a figure on horseback wearing a hood and holding a staff in his hand; pawns are represented by labourers with spade and whip, a blacksmith, a clerk, other types of worker; a man with a pair of scales and a purse on his belt; an apothecary, a spicer, a physician, innkeeper, a servant and a dice-player.

This first chapitre of the first tractate shelweth Vn, der What-kyng the playe of the Chesse was founden and maad . Capitulo Primo

Amonge alle the euyl condicions & signes that may be in a man the first and the grettest is . Whan he se, reth not ne dredeth to displese & make wroth god by synne & the peple by lyuyng disordonatly / Whan he retcheth not nor taketh hede vnto them that repreue hym and his vy, ces , But sleeth them· In suche wyse as did the emperour nero·Whiche did do slee his mayster seneque ; for as moche as he myght not suffre to be repreuyd & taught of hym . in like wise was sotyme a kyng in babilon that was named

A page from *The Book of Chess*, printed by Caxton in 1480. (*Radio Times*)

The game of chess is said to have been introduced to England from the Middle East in the reign of Edward I. One of the earliest references to chess in England is contained in the works of Lydgate, while Mrs. Paston in *The Paston Letters* says that the Lady Morley: "had no harpings or lutings during Christmas, but playing at tables and chess." Obviously it was a popular game among the nobility and the minor gentry during Caxton's lifetime. He himself probably learned something of the game while at the Court of Burgundy, as Froissart mentions that Charles V of France played chess with the Duke of Burgundy. Certainly the book on chess which gave him the idea for his own production came into his hands at Bruges.

Caxton sometimes had an irritating English habit of moralising unduly, but when applying the principles of chess to morality in everyday life, he was only adapting the theme taken up by the original author of the work, Jean de Vignay, described by the printer as "an excellent doctor of divinity, of the Order of the Hospital of St. John of Jerusalem". Caxton said that the lessons of the game of chess: "applied unto the morality of the public weal, as well of the nobles and of the common people, after the game and play of chess." He went on to assert that: "other of what estate of degree he or they stand in may see in this little book that they govern themselves as they ought to do."[9]

Delighting in odds and ends of general information in a haphazard way as distinct from any systematic gathering of knowledge would appear to have been a hobby of Caxton. In many books this desire to come up with tit-bits of information, sometimes drawn from a variety of sources, sometimes from his own experience, is apparent. In the book on chess, for example, he first describes the invention of the game in the time of a king of Babylon known as Emsmerodach, which is an unconfirmed and a much earlier version of the game's origins than generally accepted today. His second treatise is on the "office of King" and with explanations of the names and associations of some of the principal chessmen. His third treatise is on the "offices of the common people" with whom he associates the pawn.

Perhaps one of the best examples of Caxton's gifts as an editor of texts was the use he made of certain sections of the *Polychronicon* to create a separate book, entitled *Description of Britain*. In effect, by taking out those parts of the *Polychronicon* relating to the geography of the British Isles, Caxton was able to produce a very simple text-book and guide to the territory. In this book Caxton presents a picture of Britain which covers not only England, but Ireland, Scotland and Wales as well, including details of rivers, roads, cities, towns, laws and languages. Here Caxton showed little originality other than inspired editing: he might well have amended and added to what Trevisa translated from Ralph Higden. But, as Caxton had been out of the country for most of his life, his own knowledge of British geography must have been limited to what he had read and heard.

He always showed a flair for providing his readers with easily assimilable knowledge. Probably none knew better than he how few courtiers were scholars and that they needed to have information served up to them in modest doses. His selection of *The Image or Mirror of the World* was typical of Caxton in his role of the popular medieval educator of the nobility. Translated from the French, it touched on a wide range of subjects from philosophy and geography to meteorology and astronomy. But in writing the prologue for this work Caxton employed an unusual tactic in his translation. Instead of literally translating the French, as was normally his custom, he embellished and extended it. He spun out his translation almost as though he was padding out pages that had to be used up, sometimes supplying three adjectives where the French version only had one, doubling his verbs without justification and occasionally adding in some item of information of his own. The overall impression is that in his prologue to this book Caxton the editor became Caxton the public relations officer and propagandist. He was trying to sell the book, to beat the drum to win over his readers. In modern times this would be done with an emaciated preface and a punch-line at the end. In Caxton's time it was done by pattern-weaving with words, emphasising points by doubling up on nouns, adjectives and verbs, turning a simple prologue into a fugue of doublets and triplets.

He was as cautious as ever, all the same. Caxton always anticipated criticism from his readers. He was no Hugh Cudlipp who would "publish and be damned", nor a Duke of Wellington giving the come-uppance to his blackmailing mistress. Caxton's policy was to print what he felt was right to print, but to beg his readers to believe that if there was any error, it was not his, but the author from whom he was translating. Thus he wrote in this work: "If there be fault in measuring of the firmament, sun, moon or of the earth, or in any other marvels herein contained, I beseech you not to impute the fault to me, but in him that made my copy."[10] Not courageous editorship, but justifiably sound defensive tactics in medieval England.

Judging from the way in which he expanded the prologue to this book, Caxton intended it for a much wider market than the courtiers who normally comprised his customers. This was an attempt to break through to the merchants and all who were able to read and might have the money to buy books. Dedicated to Hugh Brice, the alderman of the City of London, Caxton stressed of this book: "I have made so plain that every man reasonably may understand it, if he, advisedly and attentively, read it, or hear it." For good measure, and doubtless to appeal to a more popular taste, Caxton introduced some twenty-seven woodcuts into the work, explaining that without these "it may not lightly be understood".

The illustrations were mainly diagrams of the scientific principles propounded in the book, but they also included some engravings intended to portray in an elementary fashion the subjects touched on in the work as a whole—a teacher looking at a globe and astronomical instruments; Christ holding in his hand a ball and cross; the creation of Eve who appears coming out of Adam's ribs; a mathematical teacher with a board on which numerical characters are inscribed; a geometry teacher with a pair of compasses in his hand, drawing diagrams; a female figure with a sheet of music in her hand, singing, and a man playing the flute; the symbole for astronomy is a man with a crude type of quadrant in his hand, taking a sight.

This was Caxton's first attempt at copious illustration and, whether because the work was rushed through, or whether Caxton's ability as an editor did not extend to art work, the truth is that some of the diagrams were so badly drawn in the first place that the printer put them in the wrong place.

Perhaps the most popular of Caxton's translations down the ages has been *The History of Reynard the Fox*. This legendary fable is none the less intriguing because its author is so elusive a figure. About 1255 a Brabantine minstrel translated Walter Map's *Lancelot du Lac* at the command of his master, Lodewijk van Velthem, and Jacob van Maerlant produced several romances dealing with Merlin and the Holy Grail. Among these Flemings was Willem, a shadowy figure, variously described as minstrel, poet, priest and scholar. His origins are vague and his best known work is undoubtedly *Van den Vos Reina-erde* (Reynard the Fox). One suggestion is that at some time Willem must have been a *praemonstratenser* from the Abbey of Drongen near Ghent, a cloister with estates near Hilst and Hulsterloo in 1269, but everything about the man remains uncertain as far as his native Holland is concerned. An unrelenting search of the archives of the Amsterdam University Library and all the principal libraries and museums of Holland produced no further clues. Yet such was the quality of his *Reynard the Fox* that speculation about him continues.

The work has always had a universal appeal down the centuries and it is to Caxton's credit that he recognised the popularity an English version of it would have. Nevertheless he was somewhat abashed by the satire of the work and he once again covered himself by stating: "There is no good man blamed herein; it is spoken generally; let every man take his own part as it belongeth and behoveth; and he that findeth him guilty in any deal or part thereof, let him better and amend him; and he that is verily good, I pray God keep him therein; and if any thing be said or written herein that may grieve or displease man, blame not me, but the fox, for they be his words and not mine. Praying all them that shall see this little treatise, to correct and amend where they shall find fault; for I have not added, nor minished, but have followed, as nigh as I can, my copy which was in Dutch."[11]

It is curious how, though Caxton dealt entirely with books and pamphlets, one sees him almost as an editor of a national newspaper, shaping popular taste, taking cognisance of public opinion and deciding what kind of writing sells best. This is because in the first place the printed book was in effect the first newspaper, but much more so because Caxton wrote prologues and epilogues and edited other people's works rather as an editor appeals to mass circulations. The circulation to which Caxton appealed was certainly not a mass one, and tremendously restricted. Nevertheless it was the all-important narrow market which had to be won over before any real break-through could be attempted. Caxton's greatest achievement was that he realised just how important it was.

Most early printers would have been content to satisfy the needs of the Court just as the publishers of the so-called "serious" newspapers such as *The Times* were content to fulfil their commitment to this very narrow readership right until the early 'sixties of the present century. Caxton as an editor can be compared with the role filled by Pulvermacher when he popularised the *Daily Telegraph* in the late 'thirties, or the belated editorial revolution at the *Sunday Times* in the 1960s. For Caxton in his life-time broke away from mere Court readership to the middle classes, the merchants of the City of London and others of the professional class.

Caxton had two complementary qualities: first, a respect for and deep appreciation of contemporary scholars and writers, which revealed itself in his scruples about tampering with their work; secondly, a ruthless desire to be up-to-date, to re-write and continue with other people's histories, and to bring into his work some semblance of a moral or political purpose. Caxton was not a critical or controversial historian: in this respect he was the editor intent upon accuracy, not the leader-writer aiming at putting over a point of view. He seems to have made use of several sources for his historical work and an example of his objectivity may be gleaned from his account of the death of King Richard II. He gave two accounts of how Richard died, but did not indicate which one he accepted beyond mentioning that one of the two versions was "the common opinion of Englishmen".

Yet this is not to say that Caxton lacked a critical approach as an editor. If his approach to history was hampered by inhibitions and some indecision, in tackling other works the impatience of the sub-editor peeped through and he pruned rigorously. In his translating of the *Golden Legend* and considering the additions he made to this work, he knew that the length of the original text would demand drastic cuts, not only because of the general reader who would be hopelessly bored if they were not made, but because of the need to keep down printing costs. On the other hand some cuts and omissions were made because of Caxton's orthodox religious beliefs. He would not tolerate doubts. Here the romantic in him coincided with the devout Catholic. In quite a few of his works he excised passages which might seem to savour of the unorthodox, or which could be construed as casting doubts on dogma or doctrine.

Perhaps one could sum up Caxton the editor as a "High Church Tory" with radical undertones—not an unusual combination in some ages—but at the same time a kind of "Beaverbrook" in reverse, that is to say an English patriot who believed the future prosperity of his country lay in achieving an understanding with other nations of Europe to form a bulwark against the infidel; added to which one could attribute to him some of the qualities of the popular educator which Northcliffe became and some of those robust Nonconformist principles which maintained the journalistic prowess of Robertson Nicoll. All this was somewhat of a medieval mish-mash, but sufficiently leavened to make this courageous man the first and easily the most influential of all English editors.

The Red Pale

CAXTON was faced with the problem that besets all editors ancient and modern—how to lay his hands on material worth printing. As has been seen, he solved this, partly through his experience as a Mercer in having the contacts who could provide him with books, partly through his having access to great libraries like those of the Court of Burgundy, and unquestionably through the wide circle of friends and patrons he acquired in his lifetime. But beyond this Caxton must have had to do some personal detective work in borrowing books and manuscripts, and seeking sufficient advantage to be able to retain these long enough for him to make translations.

When friends rallied round him, or when they desired him to print something for them, no doubt his task was made easier. Caxton, however, must have had to bend rules and use all his initiative to be able to hold on to manuscripts and books as long as he did. The statutes of St. Mary's College, Oxford, in the reign of Henry VI provided an example of the scarcity of books: "Let no scholar occupy a book in the library above one hour, or two hours at most, so that others shall be hindered from the use of same."

But the scarcity was superficial: it was the habit of Church librarians to give a book to each of a religious fraternity at the beginning of Lent, to be read during the year and to be returned the following Lent. In the great abbeys and major monasteries there was a room known as the *scriptorium*, where novices were employed in copying out from books, and even in that earliest of the public schools, Winchester, Warton wrote that: "one or more transcribers were hired by the founder to make books for the library. They transcribed and took their commons within the college, as appears by computations of expenses on their account now remaining."[1]

The scarcity of books led to several instances of theft among people in high places. Thus the Prior of Christ Church, Canterbury, lent a book of St. Gregory to King Henry V and he complained that after the King's death the book was taken by the Prior of Shene. The illuminated, expensively produced books of the era immediately prior to the invention of printing were desirable works of art, coveted by connoiseurs. In the wardrobe accounts of King Edward IV it is recorded that Piers Bauduyn was paid for "binding, gilding and dressing of two books" twenty shillings each, and of four books, sixteen shillings each. Twenty shillings in that period would have bought an ox. But the cost of this binding and garnishing does not stop there: for there were delivered to the binder six yards of velvet, six yards of silk, laces, tassels, copper and gilt clasps and nails.

Another example of how books were then coveted is given in some notes in French in a manuscript work given to King Edward IV entitled *Le Bible Historiaux*: "This book was taken from the King of France at the Battle of Poitiers, and the good Count of Salisbury, William Montague, bought it for a hundred marks and gave it to his Lady Elizabeth, the good Countess. . . . Which book the Countess assigned to her executors to sell for forty livres."

As a Mercer's apprentice Caxton would have undertaken the task of stamping the merchant's mark upon his master's bales, and from this he may have had the idea of printing being developed from this primitive beginning. Whatever lesson he learned from the process of stamping, it is certain that he regarded it as of the utmost importance for his book shop to have a sign. Thus, when he set up shop at the "Sign of the Red Pale" in the Almonry of Westminster Abbey, he took good care to advertise the fact, as his poster and handbill testifies.[2]

The exact date of this "advertisement" is a subject of some controversy, but 1477–1478 is that usually ascribed to it. It is this uncertainty over the exact date which led earlier writers to insist that Caxton's first press was set up in the Almonry and not in the place we have already indicated. But it seems clear that the move to the Almonry was mainly for the purpose of having a shop in which to sell the books he printed. Lawrence E. Tanner insists that: "it was not until some years later [i.e. after the setting up of the original print-shop], wither in 1482 or 1483, that he took in addition to his first shop the premises in the Almonry usually known as the Red Pale."[3]

In this period Caxton took two tenements in the Almonry at rents of ten shillings and three shillings and fourpence respectively per quarter. It is hard to believe that he required additional premises for printing after this period, yet in 1485 he took on another tenement at 13s. 4d. a year. Possibly he required the loft for the storing of books. It would be about this time that he reached the zenith of his prestige as a printer.

But there may well have been another reason for the choice of these other premises. The year 1483 saw Edward IV die, Edward V come to the throne only to be succeeded by the usurper, Richard III. A traumatic time for one so deeply committed to the Woodvilles and other opponents of Richard of Gloucester. Caxton may have felt that he might need some protection in the near future and this could well have influenced his choice of premises. The Almonry of Westminster Abbey lay apart from the main buildings of the Monastery which were grouped around the Cloister. What is today known as Dean's Yard was then called the Home Farm and surrounded by farm buildings and sheds. The Almonry was beyond the farm and the Black Ditch and was approached from the north-west corner of Dean's Yard near the present gateway by an alley which crossed the Black Ditch by a bridge. In short, the Almonry was outside the inner precincts of the monastery, but inside the sanctuary boundaries, which is perhaps the most significant point of all. Caxton may well have been seeking some kind of unwritten guarantee of sanctuary against political intrigues at the same time as he was setting up his press. In the reign of Richard III this might have been a matter of life and death.

The Almonry shop must have been intended mainly as a place for selling books and also for displaying them to passers-by and casual customers. But it is also possible that an equally important function of these premises was as a meeting place for his patrons and friends and even a modest amount of business on behalf of the State. During Richard III's reign there would not have been much of the latter, but it is quite conceivable that the Red Pale was a place for secret meetings between opponents of Richard. Old though Caxton may have been when Henry VII came to the throne, it is worth noting that the new King made various payments to Caxton and that the latter's advice and services were sought on occasions. This suggests that Caxton may have aided the allies of Henry Tudor.

It would be interesting to know if Caxton actually worked in co-operation with Otwel Fulle. If Otwel was indeed the "schoolmaster of

St. Albans", or, more accurately a master at Westminster School, then Caxton would have known all about him. Caxton's strength as a printer was that he never set himself up against other printers in an aggressive spirit: he was always eager to learn and to co-operate rather than to oppose. It would have been in keeping with Caxton's character to have collaborated with Otwel and possibly to have rendered him some assistance when Otwel ceased to print himself. Much of this must inevitably be supposition, but the Westminster Abbey Muniments reveal that Otwel Fulle was "a master of the scholars in the Almonry", and who in 1482–1483 was granted a lease of one of the five tenements within the Sanctuary built by Master Walter Cooke for the support of the singer of the Chantry which he had founded at Knowle in Warwickshire. The reference to Warwickshire is interesting: did Otwel Fulle supply Caxton with the Malory manuscript? Or did he bequeath this to Caxton in his will? Otwel Fulle died in the period 1482–1484 according to the records of the churchwardens' accounts for St. Margarets.

Lawrence Tanner provides by far the best account of the various premises which Caxton rented in Westminster and he explains how the Almonry occupied a site around the east end of what is now Victoria Street with Tothill Street as its northern boundary. It consisted of an alms-house with a hall and chapel dedicated to St. Anne, a courtyard, stables, granary and a barn. The Almoner himself was also *ex-officio* Rector of St. Margaret's. It was he who made the entry in the account roll for 1482–1483:

"De Camera sup [ra] portam exteriorem nuper de D [auid] Selley ad T [erminum] xl annorum hoc a [nn] o xxxvj jam in tenencia Willi Caxton per annum lljs iiijd."

As William Blades suggests, Caxton's association with the Mercers' Company may have had something to do with his obtaining the rental of premises at Westminster as the Mercers held certain tenements of the Abbot of Westminster. The printers of the fifteenth century, especially in Holland and Flanders, used armorial bearings for their trade marks, the shield being represented as hanging down from the branch of a tree. It has been suggested that Caxton used a shield with a broad red band down the centre. This band in the centre of the shield was known as a pale and, if painted red, would, of course, represent "The Red Pale".

In some respects Caxton can be compared to the really great film directors of this day and age. They will gladly spend years and a vast amount of money of their own in fostering one or two masterpieces, taking infinite pains to get everything right and accepting a loss in doing so, but, in order to be able to carry on, devoting much of their time to bringing out a vast number of short, commercial films. Caxton likewise printed leaflets, short poems and educational works to help pay for the major projects on which he embarked, not all of which were paid for by patrons.

One of the earliest books that came from his press was a *Book of Hours*, the *Horae* which went into four editions, almost certainly the first prayer-book printed in England and definitely the first printed on vellum. It contained only twelve lines to a full page, but was without signatures, numbers to pages or headlines. The prayers are to the Three Kings of Cologne and to St. Barbara, which suggests that the book may originally have been commissioned for Cologne merchants of the Hanseatic League in London, as their patron saint was St. Barbara.

While no serious typographical expert today would suggest that Caxton was the equal of the best continental printers, he was capable of better printing than most of them suggest. But he stuck rigidly to his principle aim—to print books which were easily readable and durable as speedily as possible. Thus, unlike the continental printers, Caxton did not use signatures for six years, while none of his books had a title page and very few had either illustrations or foliation and pagination. Towards the end of his life he speeded up his production rate, almost as though he was anticipating death.

In fourteen years Caxton printed more than 18,000 pages, mostly of folio size and nearly eighty separate books. He did most of the overseeing, though his three main assistants, Wynkyn de Worde, Richard Pynson and Robert Copland increasingly undertook the whole task of printing, giving Caxton more time to concentrate on his translation work. In all he translated twenty-one books at least from French and one from Dutch, but there may well have been many others which were never printed. Romance or romantic themes easily accounted for the bulk of his production, and significantly a number of these went into second, third and even fourth editions. There were five devotional books and one medical work.

Between 1478 and 1484 Caxton shared in the auditing of the

parochial accounts of St. Margaret's, Westminster. It seems probable that his experience as Governor of the English Nation in Bruges was called upon in this respect. It was stated that the audit was carried out "in the presence of John Randolf, squire, Richard Umpuy, gentleman, Thomas Burgeys, John Kendall, notary, William Caxton . . . with other parishioners". The parish accounts also show that the fifteen copies of his *Golden Legend*, already mentioned, were "bequothen to the Church by W. Caxston".

Some of Caxton's biographers have stated that he used the Scriptorium of the Abbey for his printing. There is no proof of this and it is exceedingly unlikely that Abbot John Esteney would have allowed it. Printing was not only still regarded as being *avant garde*, but the smells accompanying it were regarded as akin to the Devil and it was a filthy business which would have made life irksome to say the least for the scribes and translators in the Scriptorium. But it is more than likely that Caxton may have used the Scriptorium for his translation work, or consulted scribes there about his own translation problems.

Caxton's "Device", as it has been called, first appeared in those books—twelve in all—printed after 1487. The device is first seen at the end of a Sarum Missal and consists of Caxton's initials in capital letters with a strange interlacement of lines between the two letters, while near the W is a stroke resembling a small s and near the C a stroke resembling a small c. The whole is enclosed in floral borders. The central lines have been assumed to be a fantastic imprint of the figures "74" and a reference to the all important fact that in 1474 Caxton printed the first English book. This last theory seems highly improbable, as, too, does another view that this represents Caxton's age at the time. Both Henry Bradshaw, of Cambridge, and William Blades took the line that the design did not represent any Arabic numerals and Blades asserted that it bore a striking resemblance to the merchants' mark of another Mercer, one John Felde, as shown on his brass in Standon Church, Hertfordshire.

The letters s. c. may mean *sancta colonia*, referring to Cologne, which has been used by those writers who argue that Caxton always paid tribute to his printing school in Cologne rather than Bruges. But there is no confirmation of this theory. S. c. could equally stand for *scilicet* (to wit).

When the Woodvilles were removed from their positions of influ-

Printer's mark used by Caxton. (*Radio Times*)

ence, Caxton must have suffered from a scarcity of patrons, actual and prospective, among the aristocracy. It was probably for this reason that he turned to Daubney, Pratt and others. In the years immediately following the advent of Richard III he had to depend on the Mercers' Company and the City of London for patrons. It is said that on his death bed, Caxton's great friend, William Pratt, begged him to print the *Book of Good Manners*. It is more than likely that he actually provided him with the cash to do this. Caxton is said to have finished the translation of the latter book a month before his friend died in July, 1486.

Pratt's will was proved the following month, but Caxton's name is not mentioned in it. But this was the period in which, undoubtedly for political reasons and his own safety, Caxton did not name his patrons when printing his books, but referred to each one in such a way that generally speaking they could be identified.

Henry VII was the link-man, the monarch who helped England finally move out of medievalism into enlightened, inquiring, progressive Tudor England. He contrasted with his Yorkist brothers in that he was not a soldier, but one devoted to the idea of peace and progress. Prudent, far-seeing, the first economist-King, Henry was conscious of all possible plots that might be made against him and always suspicious of intrigues, sometimes when they did not even exist. Yet, as Bacon said, as he easily became apprehensive and full of suspicions: "so did he easily check them and master them. . . . He was a prince sad, serious and full of thoughts and secret observations; and full of notes and memorials of his own hand as to whom to reward, whom to inquire of, whom to beware, what were the dependencies, what were the factions and the like."[4]

It was to the Tudors in general that Britain owed the development of national espionage. Henry VII, when harried from one place to another by Richard III in the years before he came to the throne, had learned at first hand the importance of a personal espionage system. It was only through the vigilance of his own agents that he foiled a plot by Richard III to have him kidnapped in Brittany. It is possible that Caxton was one of Henry Tudor's agents, although there is no proof of this. But the recognition which Henry gave to this ageing man suggests that at some time Caxton must have been of service to him and in the field of foreign intelligence Caxton would always have been extremely knowledgeable.

Henry VII was not exactly a natural patron for Caxton to have. The King's most formidable enemy was Margaret Duchess of Burgundy, Caxton's first patron, Edward IV's sister and Henry's aunt by marriage. The Duchess made welcome any dissident Yorkists who might wish to flee from England and encouraged them to make Bruges a base for plotting against the English King.

Did Caxton keep Henry VII informed of the Duchess's intrigues? He must have been aware of them. Francis Bacon wrote that: "this princess, having the spirit of a man and malice of a woman, abounding

Henry VII, Caxton's last patron. (*Radio Times*)

in treasure by the greatness of her dower and her provident government, and being childless and without any nearer care, made it her
design and enterprise to see the majesty royal of England once again
replaced in her house."[5]

Margaret was conscious of the fact that her two brothers had been on the throne for a quarter of a century between them and that this record had only been broken by Henry Tudor. She developed an almost insane hatred of the English King. From all his contacts with the Court of Burgundy Caxton could not have failed to know about this. But the desire to develop the English language by printing had by now become the greatest aim in Caxton's life: all else was sublimated to it. Had this not been so, the probability is that we should know far more about Caxton, that he would have written more of his own views and his life. But he was determined as far as he possibly could to ensure that printing was carried on and he was quick to realise that Henry VII was far more book-minded than Richard III. Henry took a delight in adding to the royal library with printed books as well as manuscripts and he retained Quintyn Paulet, who had been Keeper of the Royal Books since 1464. It was possibly Quintyn who brought Caxton's work to the attention of Henry VII. Quintyn Paulet was a collector of rare and precious manuscripts which he lovingly cared for and often had bound in silk and velvet. Possibly Quintyn obtained for Caxton the manuscript of Christine de Pisan's *Feat of Arms and Chivalry*, which Caxton translated from the French and printed in July, 1489, though the manuscript was actually presented to him by the King through the intervention of Robert de Vere, Earl of Oxford. De Vere became one of Caxton's most important patrons in these later years.

Another patron in this same period was Margaret, Duchess of Somerset, the mother of Henry VII, at whose request Caxton translated the romance, *Blanchardin and Eglantine*. Possibly it was Margaret, rather than any of the courtiers surrounding Henry VII, who advanced Caxton's cause at Court, for he must have known her for some years before Henry came to the throne. When *Blanchardin and Eglantine* was printed Caxton in his prologue stated that the Duchess of Somerset had "long afore" bought the manuscript from him.

It was in the same year that Caxton produced his medical book— *The Governal of Health*, which was originally written in Latin, but had been translated into English before Caxton edited it for his press. The book itself is not especially noteworthy, being a hotchpotch of quotations taken from Arabian and Greek physicians and with some traces of Lydgate of all people. This was hardly one of Caxton's better books, though doubtless it had a fair circulation, as it was the earliest medical book in the English language. It is generally thought that Wynkyn de Worde persuaded Caxton to print this work.

About the same time Caxton was also printing a small volume of the *Statutes* of the reign of Henry VII. Almost certainly this commission came from the King, though indirectly the Earl of Oxford or even the Duchess of Somerset may have suggested Caxton being used for such a work, as this was a new departure for him. W. J. B. Crotch refers to the fact that payments from the royal exchequer were made to Caxton through the Privy Purse Expenses, and that such payments were for "divers appointments to be made for the See and otherwise". Caxton undoubtedly ended his days as one firmly re-established in Court circles as far as influence was concerned.[6]

But, as William Blades rightly says: "the history of Caxton after his settlement at Westminster is almost confined to a catalogue of the productions of his press." To fill in the gaps one often has to guess, to try to make accurate predictions and, after all this time, this is not always easy. That he believed he had a vital mission to perform before he died and that he needed time to complete it is clear from many things—his refusal to take life more quietly as he got older, his stepping-up of plans for the future, the fact that in June, 1490, when *Eneydos* was produced, he was still seeking long-term backing at Court. For it was then that he presented to the sickly child, Prince Arthur, heir to the throne, his adaptation of Virgil's verse. Did Caxton believe, as he might well have done, that to ensure that England never forgot print-ing, he needed to produce much more and extend the circulation of his works? Did he expect to live much longer? For in 1490 Arthur was a mere four years old. Or was it Caxton's romanticism which stirred him to hope that at long last the age of chivalry was to return to England in the image of a King-to-be who was named after the mythical monarch of ancient legend?

Arthur, of course, never came to the throne, and, had he done so, probably far too much would have been expected of him, as the legend of the fabulous Arthur and his links with Cadwallader, ancestor of Henry VII, were carefully fostered by the Tudors. Arthur died on 2 April, 1502, having been married to Catherine of Aragon when she was a girl of fifteen and he was nine months younger. Catherine insisted afterwards that the marriage was never consummated.

Arthur's tutor was John Skelton, who was one of the outstanding literary critics of his day, a scholar who had delved deeply into the writings of classical scholars past and present and who was an authority on style in literature. Skelton may have advised Caxton, but without question Caxton introduced Skelton's name into the prologue to *Eneydos*.

To understand how Caxton, to the end of his days, had to cope not merely with the problems of winning and holding patrons, finding and holding and even increasing the number of his customers, but with the formidable hazards which printing presented to him, one cannot do better than quote from Charles Knight, who wrote at a period of the early nineteenth century when printing was still relatively primitive and there would be a much keener appreciation of the kind of problems with which Caxton was faced. Knight writes:

"A famous printer, Jodocus Badius Ascensianus, has exhibited his press in the title-page of a book printed by him in 1498. Up to the middle of the last century this rude press was in use in England; although the press of an ingenious Dutch mechanic, Blaew, in which the pressure was rapidly communicated from the screw to the types, and all the parts of the press were yielding so as to produce a sharp but not a crushing impression, was gradually superseding it. The early printers manufactured their own ink, so that Caxton had to learn the art of ink-making. The ink was applied to the types by balls, or dabbers, such as one of the men holds who is working the press of Badius. Such dabbers were universally used in printing thirty years ago. As the ancient weaver was expected to make his own loom, so, even this short time since, the division of labour was so imperfectly applied to printing that the pressman was expected to make his own balls. A very rude and nasty process it was. The sheep-skins, called pelts, were prepared in the printing office, where the wool with which they were stuffed was also carded; and these balls, thus manufactured by a man whose general work was entirely of a different nature, required the expenditure of at least half an hour's labour every day in a very disagreeable operation, by which they were kept soft.

"There were many other little niceties in the home construction of the materials for printing which Caxton would necessarily have to learn. But in the earlier stages of an art requiring such nice arrangements, both in the departments of the compositor, or setter-up of type, and of the pressman, it is quite clear that many things which, by the habit of four centuries, have become familiar and easy in a printing-office, would be exceedingly difficult to be acquired by the first printers. Rapidity in the work was probably out of the question. Accidents must constantly have occurred in wedging up the single letters tightly in pages and sheets; and when one looks at the regularity of the inking of these old books, and the beautiful accuracy with which the line on one side (called by the printers 'register'), we may be sure that with very imperfect mechanical means an amount of care was taken in working off the sheets which would appear ludicrous to a modern pressman. The higher operation of a printing-office, which consists in reading the proofs, must have been in the first instance full of embarrassment and difficulty. A scholar was doubtless employed to test the accuracy of the proofs, probably someone who had been previously employed to overlook the labours of the transcribers. Fierce must have been the indignation of such a one during a course of painful experience, when he found one letter presented for another, letters and even syllables and words omitted, letters topsy-turvy and even actual substitutions of one letter for another. These are almost unavoidable consequences of the mechanical operation of arranging moveable types, so entirely different from the work of the transcriber.

"The corrector of the press would not understand this and his life would not be a pleasant one. Caxton was no doubt the corrector of his own press, and well for him it was that he brought to his task the patience, industry and good temper which are manifest in his writings."[7]

But a printer in Caxton's time had many other problems with which to cope. He had to be a bookbinder as well as a printer. The board, literally a wooden board, between which the leaves were fastened, was as thick as a thin panel of wood. The finished book was a weighty affair with large brass nails with ornamental heads on the outside of the cover and magnificent corners and clasps. It was made to last for many years, if not indefinitely. Erasmus said of such a book that "no man can carry it about, much less get it into his head."

These books, though printed in very small numbers, did last sufficiently to help sustain the English literary revolution of the sixteenth century. By the time Shakespeare was turning out his plays the effects of Caxton became plain for all to see. It is not difficult to see that Shakespeare had been inspired by Caxton. In *The Histories of Troy* Caxton recorded that: "Andromeda saw that night a marvellous vision and it seemed that if Hector went into battle that day he would be slain. And she, that had great fear and dread of her husband, weeping, said to him, praying that he would not go to the battle that day;

whereof Hector blamed his wife, saying that she should not believe nor give faith to dreams, and would not abide nor tarry therefore."

The Shakespearian version of this in *Troilus and Cressida* was:

"Andromache (Andromeda): 'When was my lord so much ungently temper'd,
   To stop his ears against admonishment?
   Unarm, unarm, and do not fight today.'
Hector: 'You train me to offend you; get you gone:
   By the everlasting gods I'll go.'
Andromache: 'My dreams will, sure, prove ominous to the day.'
Hector: 'No more, I say.'"

There are glimpses of Caxton's inspiration in *A Midsummer's Night Dream* and again in Spenser's *Fairy Queen*. In the latter's description of the gate of the Bower of Bliss there is more than a mere hint of Caxton:

"It framed was of precious ivory,
That seemed a work of admirable wit;
And therein all the famous history
Of Jason and Medea was ywrit;
Her mighty charms, her furious loving fit;
His goodly conquest of the golden fleece,
His falsed faith, and love too lightly flit;
The wonder'd Argo, which in venturous peace
First through the Euxine Seas bore all the flower
   of Greece."

Compare this with Caxton's prologue to *The Book of Jason*: ". . . But well wot I that the noble Duke Philip, first founder of this said order, did so maken a chamber in the Castle of Hesdyn, wherein was craftily and curiously depainted the conquest of the Golden Fleece by the said Jason. In which chamber I have been and seen the said history so depainted, and in remembrance of Medea, and of her cunning and science, he had made in the said chamber, by subtil engine, that, when he would, it should seem that it lightened, and after thunder, snow and rain, and all within the said chamber, as oft times and when it should please him, which was made for his singular pleasure. Then for the honour and worship of our said most redoubted liege lord, which hath taken the said order, I have under the shadow of his noble protection enterprised to accomplish this said little book."

Whether or not the "Mawde Caxton" who was buried at Westminster in 1490 was the printer's wife, it is not without some significance either of his wife's death or his own approaching end that in this same year Caxton started to edit *The Art and Craft to Die Well*. This book was printed without the printer's name, the place or date, though the latter was almost certainly 1491. We know that Caxton translated it sometime in 1490 from a French edition by Verard in Paris of a Latin work of much earlier date. French translations of the work had previously been printed in Paris and Bruges where Colard Mansion was the printer.

Towards the end of his life Caxton had turned more to books of religious significance. There was the *Fifteen Oes*, a quarto volume of prayers, each prayer beginning with an "O", a work which was commissioned by Margaret Duchess of Somerset. This was the only book of Caxton's which was ornamented with wood-cut borders. These borders were crude, but nonetheless fascinating examples of an early art, each border consisting of four pieces and eight separate sets of designs were used throughout the book. The decorative emblems included spirals of flowers and foliage, birds, animals and occasionally a grotesque human figure such as one saw on church gargoyles. The book was also notable for a full-page cut out of the Crucifixion.

Exactly when Caxton died is uncertain, but it was almost certainly sometime during 1491, or at latest early 1492. On 15 June, 1490, he had finished translating *The Art and Craft to Die Well*, seemingly cutting short the beginning of this book in this manner: "When it is so, that, what a man maketh or doeth, it is made to come to some end, and if the thing be good and well made it must needs come to good end; then by better and greater reason every man ought to intend in such wise to live in this world, in keeping the commandments of God, that he may come to a good end, And then out of this world, full of wretchedness and tribulations, he may go to heaven unto God and his saints unto joy perdurable."

The words were prophetic. Whatever was the cause of Caxton's death, whether it was sudden or long anticipated, he kept going to the last. According to Wynkyn de Worde, he had just completed a translation of the *Lives of the Fathers* when he died. Wynkyn himself later printed this work and in his own edition he states that the book was: "translated out of French into English by William Caxton of Westminster, late dead, and finished it at the last day of his life."

In the churchwardens' accounts of the parish of St. Margaret of Westminster there is the following item covering the period 1491–1492:

> "Atte bureyng of William Caxton for
> iiij torches   vj^s viiij^d
> Item for the belle at same bureyng   vj^d"

William Blades gave his opinion that, judging from the position of this item in the parochial accounts, it would seem that Caxton died towards the end of 1491. Blades goes on to assert that "this date is confirmed by the following manuscript note, quoted by Ames: 'There is wrote down in a very old hand in a *Fructus Temporum* of my friend Mr. Ballard's, of Cambden, in Gloucestershire—*Of your charitee pray for the soul of Mayster Wyllyam Caxton, that in hys time was a man of muche ornate and moche renommed wysdome and connyn, and deceased ful crystenly the yere of our Lord MCCCCLXXXX J.*' "[8]

Blades also pointed out that the fees mentioned in the parochial accounts were "considerably higher than those paid by the majority of the parishioners and are equalled in but very few instances; they thus afford further evidence of the superior position held by our printer in his parish."

When death came to Caxton he must have been about seventy years of age. It is almost certain that he had planned things so that Wynkyn de Worde would take over his business and carry on the printing tradition. No doubt arrangements to this end were completed before Caxton died so that nothing depended on his will. This appears to be borne out by the fact that Wynkyn de Worde began to pay for Caxton's tenements immediately after his death.

The Development of the English Press

HILE any biography of Caxton must of necessity be a sparse and insubstantial work through sheer lack of vital evidence about his life, it would be an insensitive biographer who would merely put a full stop after the mention of his death.

"The evil that men do lives after them, the good is oft interred with their bones," wrote Shakespeare, but with Caxton the reverse was true. Nobody must have planned more carefully than he what was to happen after his death. There is no trace of his will, yet it is assumed that he made one. Caxton, one cannot help suspecting, was less concerned about his will as with ensuring that printing was carried on in England, that the torch he had so bravely lit and carried through difficult times and during four reigns, would be handed on to others. He was determined that the power of the printed word should be extended. No doubt this intensely religious man fully realised from his study of history how England had been plunged into an oblivion of the spirit in the Dark Ages. This was why he carried on with his translations if one accepts the testimony of Wynkyn de Worde, right up to the day of his death. This is why he ensured that before he died all arrangements were completed for Wynkyn de Worde to carry on his printing press and that Richard Pynson and Robert Copland should assist him.

Henry Plomer remarked: "that the printing-press would sooner or later have been established in England is certain, but it is well for the country that it was brought over by such a man as William Caxton, who put the fear of God and the good of his country before all other considerations, and who laid on a solid foundation the road which has led us to such high and noble results."[1]

This may sound like a gilding over of the blunt testimony of Caxton himself that he was a printer in order to make a livelihood, but it is a strong possibility that unless Caxton had planned for the future of his press after his death, the development of the English language would have been slowed down. Just as printing presses disappeared at a day's notice on the continent so could the same have happened in England, and as Caxton was the sole printer in the English language, such a closure as that of the press at the Red Pale could have retarded the new learning by a whole decade or more.

Wynkyn de Worde kept his promise to Caxton that he would print the *Lives of the Fathers*. This book came off the press in 1495, duly signed with the words: "Wynkyn de Worde this hath set in print in William Caxton's house."

It was Wynkyn de Worde who encouraged his assistants to go ahead and print on their own. They were fearful that if there was an increase in the number of printing presses in England, competition would drive them all out of business. Wynkyn argued that whereas in the early days of Caxton's press a printer depended absolutely on the nobility, by the end of the 1490's a new market was opening up—that of the merchants, the grocers and small traders of the City of London, and even in the taverns minstrels clamoured for the printed ballad.

Wynkyn de Worde did not show much enterprise on his own account in Caxton's lifetime, but this was probably due to his intense loyalty to his master. In his early days as Caxton's successor he kept closely to his master's methods and choice of texts, but gradually he branched out and published more popular works. He improved the quality of his paper and type-faces, introduced title-pages and began to cater for a middle-class market. It was probable the change in the type of customer which caused him to move to Fleet Street in 1500. Wynkyn de Worde lived until 1535 and this friend and assistant of Caxton turned out more than 400 books, a remarkable effort even if it extended over forty-two years, which means he averaged ten books a year. He paid tribute to Caxton even in the device he adopted, incorporating something of Caxton's own device and initials in his own.[2]

Richard Pynson, whose printing activities covered the years 1493–1531, was a native of Normandy who became an assistant of Caxton for some years, referring to the latter in his preface to the works of Chaucer as "my worshipful master". Pynson not only carried on printing on his own account, but became the first King's Printer, for which post he received a small salary. He printed more than 200 books.

Robert Copland joined Wynkyn de Worde and assisted him until Wynkyn's death, after which he set up on his own. Though he carried on the trade of printing for a longer period than any other in the fifteenth century and well into the sixteenth, only eleven books are actually credited to him.

Other printers who began to make their appearance early in the sixteenth century were William Faques (1502–1508), Henry Pepwell (1505–1539) and Peter Treveris (1514–1531). Not one of these achieved any great distinction and it is clear that the pioneer work of printing was mainly carried on by Copland, Wynkyn de Worde and Pynson after Caxton's death.[3]

As the sixteenth century got under way, there was an increasing demand for cheap copies of the ancient classics, though the early English printers did little to fulfil this. Up to the year 1540 not a single Greek book came from an English press. Relatively little was done in Latin either. But gradually English dictionaries, grammar books, primers and Catechisms began to appear in profusion, and perhaps an even greater influence was when John Rastell, the friend and printer of Sir Thomas More, translated and abridged the Statutes, most of which were written in French, at last enabling the English people to understand their own laws.[4]

Thus the printing-press created the fastest and, in its early days at least, the most peaceable revolution ever known. It was helped on its progress—admittedly slower in some ways than that of the continent —by the fact that as there were so few printers in England, they did not make competition too fierce. Most printers belonged to the Stationers' Company, which had developed from the medieval Guild of Scriveners, Limners (Illuminators), Bookbinders and Stationers. Despite restrictive practices aimed at protecting the individual printer and the fact that printers were few in number, it was still hard to make a living at this trade even in the early sixteenth century. This perhaps is in itself a tribute to Caxton's business acumen. Indeed, the situation for printers was serious enough for them to press for legislation, eventually passed, protecting them from foreign-born printers who came to London to compete with them. In 1555 Parliament banned foreign printers altogether, unfortunately ensuring that the standard of English printing remained far below that of the continent.

Richard Grafton was the first publisher of an English Bible in 1537 in collaboration with his partner, Whitchurch, though the printing was done in Zurich. Three years later Grafton published Cranmer's Bible, the first actually to be printed in England. Yet even the diligent Grafton produced fewer books than Caxton, his total being only ninety.

But the quantity of copies per book being then turned out was much greater. The doctrines of the Reformation had seeped through into the country and had considerable impetus from Henry VIII's quarrel with the Church of Rome. There was, of course, hostility in many quarters to the printing of an English Bible and many were burnt. The sales were substantial enough to pave the way for more Bibles to be printed and the burning of them was perhaps the best publicity the Bible could get. In 1540 Grafton printed only 500 copies of his complete edition of the Scriptures, yet between 1526 and 1600 no fewer than 326 editions of the Bible, or parts of the Bible, were turned off the press.

There is, however, one interesting contrast between the post-Caxton printers and Caxton himself. Until the beginning of the seventeenth century no printer emerged with a stature, or a comparably efficient approach to his task, to equal that of Caxton himself. This is not to deride, or denigrate, in any way the admirable printers who followed him. But it was Caxton who in those early, extremely difficult years, when England was riddled with factionalism, kept his hand firmly on the tiller and guided printing from the shallows of self-destruction, in which so many had foundered, and at the same time set himself up as a guide and arbiter to the new future of books.

Caxton's experience as merchant, diplomat and negotiator stood him in good stead in this respect. He did not have to contend with the threat of censorship which beset later printers. The Stationers' Company, of which Caxton was always suspicious, made one of its chief tasks that of guarding the nation against alleged sedition. By 1538 all books had to be licensed, and in 1586 a decree of the Star Chamber restricted the number of printers in London to 25 and gave the Stationers' Company powers to raid their premises and seize material and presses, if necessary.

It was in his prologues and epilogues that Caxton showed his stature. There is no doubt that he regarded these as being of paramount importance, combining an introduction to the work being produced with a dedication, an explanation and an advertisement, and very often with a modicum of moralising and advice thrown in for good measure. The importance Caxton attached to the prologues and epilogues can be gauged from the fact that while in many instances a work he was translating already had a prologue or epilogue, sometimes there was none at all. It was then that Caxton would himself fill the gap. When it came either merely to translating the prologues and epilogues of others, adapting or amending them, adding to them, or even composing an original one, Caxton revealed himself as a man with a mission. His self-imposed task was to advertise in every possible way the benefits which printing offered, to explain the purpose of publishing a book and the advantages which might accrue to its readers, and also to anticipate criticism by making it absolutely clear where a book had a passage missing, or where details needed to be filled in, or where there were real problems in the translation.

Caxton was in effect a schoolmaster for adults. A *village* schoolmaster, perhaps, and not a scholar. But what shone through all his adulation of the nobility, all his flattery of patrons was an instinctive and quite remarkable sense of integrity. However much he may have needed to switch his allegiance from one side to another in maintaining favour at the Court, Caxton never lost sight of the fact that above all the factional disputes which tore England apart at the time, the great need, perhaps even the subconscious great heart cry, of the English people as a whole was for the raising of their language from the conglomeration of disparate dialects, which existed, to standards worthy of a civilised, national community.

Those who have criticised Caxton for being an inferior translator should bear in mind that, during his life as a printer, he was waging a battle against time. He was intent on keeping his name before his potential readers, knowing full well, as any author of today appreciates, that if he missed a year or two in producing books, he would swiftly be forgotten. We can still only set a rough estimate of 106 books printed by Caxton—there may even have been more—but of these he himself translated at least twenty-eight, possibly thirty. This could not have given him much opportunity for that careful revision which is the prerequisite of sound translation. But conscientious as Caxton was, anxious always to admit the possibility of mistake and even to apologise to his readers, he never lost sight of the fact that it was more important to maintain production than to achieve perfection.

In one sense Caxton was the first of the Puritans in that he seemed to believe that all art should be didactic, that if literature did not instruct and edify, it was all worthless. He was always pausing to preach, doubtless an irritating habit to those of us used to centuries of preachings and cajolings by clergy and politicians, but no doubt refreshing and well heeded in the Middle Ages. In his preface to *The Doctrinal of Sapience* Caxton stated: "this that is written in this little book ought the priests to learn and teach to their parishes; and also it is necessary for simple priests that understand not the Scriptures: and it is made for simple people and put in English. And by cause that for to hear examples stirreth and moveth the people, that ben simple, more to devotion than to that great authority of science—as it appeareth by the right reverend father and doctor Bede, priest, which saith in the Histories of England, that a bishop of Scotland, a subtle and a great clerk, was sent by the clerks of Scotland into England for to preach the Word of God, but because he used in his sermon subtle authorities, such as [for] simple people had, nor took, no savour, he returned without doing of any great good ne profit, wherefore they sent another of less science; the which was more plain, and used commonly in his sermons examples and parables by which he profited much more unto the erudition of the simple people than did that other."

In this statement and in many similar, in other prologues and epilogues, Caxton emphasised his real mission in life—that, through printing in the English language, and in developing that language while still retaining simplicity of expression, he believed a happier, more literate, more civilised and cultured people would be created.

It is perfectly true that in composing his own prologues and epilogues Caxton frequently indulged in borrowing from other men's works, but this was done more to embellish than to plagiarize. Some of this borrowed material came from French sources, others from Chaucer and Lydgate, but out of such artificial contrivances often emerged thoughts and phrases which were clearly Caxton's own. He never quite matched up to the ornateness of his contemporaries, French or English, and his stylistic accomplishments were limited. Yet, despite these defects, he never failed to drive home his message, crude though that often might be. Caxton, once he had escaped from the stranglehold of the courteous and artificial verbiage of the dedication, was as effective as a seventeenth century tract-writer or pamphleteer in some of his prologues. Indeed, it is probable that the printers and writers of the seventeenth century owed him more than those of the sixteenth. For in the half century which followed Caxton's death books still remained the luxury of the rich. In the Privy Purse accounts of Elizabeth of York, published by Sir Harry Nicolas, it was stated that in 1505, twenty pence were paid for a Primer and a Psalter. That amount of money would have bought a load of barley: it was also equal to the pay for six days' work by a labourer.[5] Nine years later *Fitzherbert's Abridgement*, a law book, was sold for forty shillings, which at that time would have bought three fat oxen.

After the Restoration an Act of Parliament was passed that only twenty printers should practice in England and in 1666 there were only 140 "working printers" in the whole of London. In the Fire of London in that year booksellers living around St. Paul's Cathedral lost a huge quantity of stock, estimated by Evelyn to amount to £200,000. The whole number of books printed during the fourteen years from 1666 to 1680 was 3,350, of which 947 were works on divinity, 420 were law books and 153 medical books.

The pamphleteers and tract-writers provided the impetus for the creation of newspapers and magazines in Britain. In this respect England did not lag far behind the continental printers. In 1644 the Swedish official journal, *Post och Inrikes Tidningar* was founded and so became the first printed newspaper in the world, to be succeeded by the *Haarlems Dagblad/Oprechte Haarlemsche Courant*, published in Haarlem in Holland in 1656. The first newspaper in the United Kingdom was that of *Berrow's Worcester Journal* which was started in 1690, while the *Stamford Mercury* is reputed to have been founded five years later and was certainly in existence in 1714. The *London Gazette*, which comes into rather a different category, and which was originally named the *Oxford Gazette*, was first published on 16 November, 1665. It is worth noting that in November, 1845 it became the most expensive daily newspaper ever sold in Britain, being sold at 2s. 8d. a copy, a sum probably equivalent to more than a pound today.

Prior to the starting up of newspapers the only form in which news was served up to the public was in "intelligence pamphlets"—rather like those privately sponsored news letters of the 1930's such as the *King Hall Letter*—which began to appear for the first time during the Civil War. Provincial newspapers established themselves more securely than most in the Metropolis in the early part of the eighteenth century.

Edward Cave made an innovation when he launched the *Gentleman's Magazine*, aimed at the wealthier middle class, yet when he offered a share in it to London booksellers, they totally rejected the plan. This was in 1731 and the *Gentleman's Magazine* was such a swift success that in the following year the very booksellers who had turned down Cave's plan started a rival magazine, *The London*.

Yet it was only after George III came to the throne that the demand for popular literature in Britain rapidly increased. Smollett's *History of England* was one of the great successes, selling up to 20,000 copies. The *Modern Catalogue of Books* from 1792–1802 shows that 4,096 new works were published, exclusive of reprints not altered in price and also exclusive of pamphlets, which meant an average of 372 new books a year, a figure far below the current 20,000 plus, but a sure sign that printing had become a successful and flourishing business.

An interesting commentary was made by a Mr. McCulloch in his *Commercial Dictionary* of 1843: "From inquiries we have made with much care and labour, we find that at an average of the four years ending with 1842, 2,149 volumes of new books, and 755 volumes of new editions and reprints (exclusive of pamphlets and periodical publications) were annually published in Great Britain; and we have further ascertained that the publication price of the former was 8s. 9½ and of the latter 8s. 2d. a volume. Hence, if we suppose the average impression of each work to have been 750 copies, it will be seen that the total value of the new works annually produced, if they were sold at their publication price, would be £708,498 8s. 9d., and that of the new editions and reprints £231,218 15s. We believe, however, that if we estimate the price at which the entire impressions of both descriptions of works actually sells at 4s. a volume, we shall not be far from the mark; and if so, the real value of the books annually produced will be £435,600 a year."

In Charles Knight's research into the development of printing and publishing in the eighteenth and early nineteenth centuries he makes an interesting contrast with the situation in the early days of printing. Citing that there were 447 newspapers in the British Isles of 1843 and that the average price of these papers was about fivepence, he remarks: "The sum annually expended in newspapers is about £1,250,000. The quantity of paper required for the annual supply of these newspapers is 121,184 reams, some of which paper is of an enormous size. In a petition to the Pope in 1471 from Sweynheim and Pannartz, printers at Rome, they bitterly complain of the want of demand for their books, their stock amounting to 12,000 volumes; and they say, 'You will admire how and where we could procure a sufficient quantity of paper, or even rags, for such a number of volumes.' About 1,200 reams of paper would have produced all the poor printers' stock. Such are the changes of four centuries."

Knight gave these estimated annual returns of the commerce of the press:

	£
New books and reprints	435,600
Weekly publications, not newspapers	100,000
Monthly publications	300,000
Newspapers	1,250,000
	2,085,600

Charles Knight himself was one who quite consciously carried the torch of Caxton into the nineteenth century. Running his own publishing company in Ludgate Street, one of his most popular publications was *The Penny Cyclopaedia of the Society for the Diffusion of Useful Knowledge*, complete in twenty-seven volumes at £10 in cloth boards, or in fourteen volumes, Half Russia, at twelve guineas. The name of the *Penny Cyclopaedia* was derived from its original issue in a weekly sheet, when a work of much less magnitude had been contemplated. From the beginning it had been supported by a great body of contributors, eminent in their respective departments. In the publisher's blurb it stated that: "the character of the work has gradually surmounted the prejudices which were excited in some quarters by its title; and the word 'Penny' is now received as indicative only of its extreme cheapness. Every article in the work is an original contribution, paid for at a rate to secure, as far as payment is concerned, the highest talent and knowledge, not only of this country, but of foreign states. The literary expenditure alone upon each volume has exceeded £1,200, making a total of £33,000. In addition, the work is fully illustrated with woodcuts, the cost of which has amounted to more than £8,000, making a total cost, for literature and art, of more than £40,000. *The Penny Cyclopaedia* may therefore, as a standard work, enter into competition, in the great essentials of fulness and accuracy, with any existing *Cyclopaedia*, whatever may be its selling price."[6]

This publication marked the beginning of a lengthy boom period of popular education that flowered from Charles Knight's *Cyclopaedia* to Harmsworth's *Encyclopaedia* and Cassel's *Popular Educator* in the early nineteenth century. Though similar projects are still published, but usually more specialised, it is extremely doubtful if anywhere in the world such an effective medium of the printing press exists today to provide so comprehensive and detailed a service at the same low cost as the *Penny Cyclopaedia*.

On this note one might usefully conclude this summary of the development of the British press in the light of Caxton's inspiration. For it was in the beginning of the nineteenth century that there occurred a revival of interest in Caxton. Prior to this nobody had seriously attempted a life of the man. Curiously, neither Pynson, Wynkyn de Worde or Copland left any detailed memoranda on Caxton's life and their combined intelligence on the subject could have been worth a good deal to any biographer of Caxton. But in 1800 the Roxburghe Club erected a tablet in Caxton's memory in St. Margaret's, Westminster. Then in 1801 the great window was added to the upper end of the hall of the Stationers' Company. The beautiful north window pictured Caxton and Edward IV and was presented to the Company by Joshua Whitehead Butterworth in 1894. Another window depicted Caxton separately.

Many libraries began to adorn themselves with paintings and statues of Caxton, a notable one being the Guildhall Library where each spandrel of the arcade has a sculptured head, including one of the printer, while the Victoria and Albert Museum has a statue of Caxton among several others on the exterior of the building. There is, however, no authentic portrait of Caxton in existence and, as Blades states, "although two or three have been published, they are all apocryphal." He adds that the only one which has any appearance of probability is the small defaced illumination in the manuscript of *Dictes and Sayings* which is in Lambeth Palace. This is the picture from which most paintings of Caxton have been copied or based. It shows King Edward IV on his throne, with the Prince of Wales (to whom Earl Rivers was tutor) by his side and two kneeling figures, one of whom is Rivers, as he is presenting to the King a copy of his translation, and the other is an

Earl Rivers presenting his Book & Caxton his Printer to Edw 4. the Queen & Prince, from a curious M.S. in the Archbishop's Library at Lambeth. The Portrait of the Prince (afterw.ᵈˢ Edw.5.ᵗʰ) is the only one known of him, & has been engraved by Vertue among the Heads of the Kings. The Person in a Cap & Robe of State is probably Richard D. of Gloucester, as he resembles the King, and as Clarence was always too great an Enemy of the Queen to be distinguished by her Brother. The Book was printed in 1477. when Clarence was in Ireland, & in the beginning of the next Year he was murder'd.

Earl Rivers presenting Caxton's book to King Edward IV in 1477. It has been claimed that Caxton is kneeling beside Earl Rivers, but the figure is that of Haywarde, Earl Rivers' transcriber. (*Radio Times*) unidentified person who for many years was named by some historians and others as being Caxton. But this was almost certainly wishful thinking by those who desired at all costs to have some portrait of the printer. Later authorities from William Blades to N. F. Blake all insist that the unidentified second figure is probably that of Haywarde, the scribe who copied out Earl Rivers' translation. The other figures are all easily identifiable by their dress, their plate-mail or coats of arms. The person next to Rivers would appear to be a monk, judging by his dress, and he has a tonsure. A manuscript in the Lambeth Palace Library would seem to confirm that the person must be Haywarde and not Caxton, as it contains a transcript of Earl Rivers' translation of the *Dictes and Sayings* written by the scribe Haywarde.

Dr. Dibdin, commenting on the alleged portrait of Caxton used in the eighteenth century biography of the printer by the Rev. John Lewis, wrote: "A portrait of Burchiello, the Italian poet, from an octavo edition of his work on Tuscan poetry, of the date 1554, was inaccurately copied by Faithorne for Sir Hans Sloane, as the portrait of Caxton." This "portrait" was touched up in Lewis' work and given a beard.[7]

In 1883 a stained glass window was set up in Westminster Abbey in honour of Caxton by the London printers. It was placed at the east end of the south aisle and there was emblazoned on it an inscription by Lord Tennyson in his most uninspired mood. Perhaps there was a feeling that Caxton might have been honoured more suitably both in the written word and in other ways. To commemorate the assistance given by the Press to the Westminster Abbey Appeal Fund, in November, 1954, a memorial tablet to Caxton was unveiled outside the south or Poets' Corner door of the Abbey, bearing this inscription:

"Near this place William Caxton set up the first printing press in England. This stone was placed here to commemorate the great assistance rendered to the Abbey Appeal Fund by the English-speaking Press throughout the world, 1954."

Supplementary Notes to Chapters

CHAPTER 1

1. *The Recuyell of the Histories of Troy,* 1474 (?).
2. *Eneydos,* trans. by Caxton, 1490. This is a translation into English from a French paraphrased version of Virgil's *Aeneid.*
3. *The Biography of William Caxton,* William Blades.
4. Letter from Mr. Nigel Nicolson to the author, 23 Oct., 1974.
5. *The Biography of William Caxton,* Blades.
6. *The Life of the Noble & Christian Prince, Charles the Great,* 1485.
7. *Miscellanies of Kent,* no. xlv, 1763.
8. The charters referring to the Caxtons are now in the British Museum. For fuller details see *The Proceedings of the Suffolk Institute of Archaeology,* xxix, 2 (1962), and also xxx, 1 (1964).

CHAPTER 2

1. This entry occurs in a list of fees for the binding and enrolment of apprentices in the Archives of the Mercers' Company.
2. Richard Whittington was never knighted even though he became Lord Mayor of London on four occasions. The title "Sir" has been given to him in various biographies, but it is inaccurate. The library which Whittington gave to the Guildhall was dispersed by the Duke of Somerset during the reign of Edward VI. In his will Whittington decreed that he left such "good or rare books [as] may seem necessary to the common library at Guildhall, for the profit of students there, and those discoursing to the common people".
3. Coster is said to have lived from about 1370 until about 1440. The quality of early Dutch type and printing is markedly inferior to that of the Germans of a slightly later period, but it may well be an undated proof or the fact that printing began in Holland. The earliest established date for printing in Holland is 1473.
4. From the *London Lickpenny,* by John Lydgate, a kind of poetic encyclopaedia and guide to London. Lydgate was born about 1370.
5. More usually known as *Caton (the Morals of Cato)* a translation from the French by Caxton, 1481.
6. *Canterbury Tales,* 2nd edition, 1484.
7. *Th'ystorye and lyf of the noble and crysten prynce, Charles the grete,* trans. from the French by Caxton, 1485.
8. *Caxton & His World,* N. F. Blake.

CHAPTER 3

1. A complete transcript of Caxton's will dated 11, April, 1441, is given in the Frederick Muller edition of William Blades' *The Biography & Typography of William Caxton* (see appendix), published 1971.

2. *The Life of Mayster Wyllyam Caxton of the Weald of Kent*, by the Rev. John Lewis, 1737.

3. *History of Troy*, trans. of *Le Recueil des histoires de Troyes*, 1475–1476.

4. *William Caxton: First English Printer:* Charles Knight.

5. The document from which this quotation is taken is to be found in one of the many volumes of Records preserved in the Archives of the City of Bruges. A full translation of the document is given in the appendix to the Frederick Muller edition of Blades' *William Caxton*, pub. 1971.

6. See *Rymer's Foedera*, London, 1710, vol. XI, 536. A translation of the document, which is headed *Concerning The Treaty of Burgundy* shows that the King at Wycombe on 20 Oct., 1464, "inasmuch as determinate arrangements concerning the intercourse of merchandise between our subjects and the subject of our well-beloved Cousin the Duke of Burgundy have in a sure form and manner been accorded and agreed to in times past and since that time often renewed, We, wishing on our part to hold good and observe such arrangements, and being well assured of the faithfulness and discretion of our well-beloved subjects Richard Whitehill, Knight, and William Caxton, Do make, ordain and constitute, by these presents, the said Richard and William our true and accredited Ambassadors, Agents, Nuncios and several Deputies. . . ."

CHAPTER 4

1. Much of the diplomatic activity and negotiations which surrounded all the treaty-making between London and Bruges took place at or near St. Omer. Letters to and from Caxton at this time were frequent and they are recorded in the Archives of the Mercers' Company. Negotiations lasted until November, 1467, before a new commercial treaty was signed.

2. See *Mémoires*, by Philippe de Commines, edited by Calmette & Durville, 3 vols., Paris, 1924–1925.

3. *Ibid.*

4. *Ibid.*

5. From the *Paston Letters*, a series of letters written to or by the Pastons, John and Margaret, a famous Norfolk family, between 1422–1509.

6. *Ibid.*

7. John Bagford collected material for a biography of Caxton in the early 18th century, but the work was never published. This material is now in the British Museum, MS. Harley 5919.

8. See preface to *The Recuyell of the Histories of Troy*.

9. *Caxton & His World*, N. F. Blake.

10. *Mémoires,* Philippe de Commines.
11. *Ibid.*

CHAPTER 5

1. See *The Book of the Order of Chivalry.* The references to the "Code of Chivalry" mentioned throughout this book are obtained from Léon Gautier's study of the literature of chivalry, out of which he worked out what he called *The Decalogue or the Ten commandments of the Code of Chivalry.*
2. See *English Social History: A Survey of Six Centuries,* G. M. Trevelyan.
3. See *Charles the Great,* Caxton.
4. This is a controversial translation of Caxton's English. It has been given as "go to the bayns [baths] and play at dice", but "bagnios" is more likely the word intended by Caxton. In fact, the baths were often a form of bagnio.
5. The Golden Fleece was founded in 1430 by Philip the Good, Duke of Burgundy, and was recognised as the most coveted order of knighthood in Europe after that of the Garter. Its name was partly inspired by the fact that the fleece or sheep-wool represented the wealth and prosperity of Burgundy and by the legend of Jason and the Golden Fleece.
6. See *William Caxton: First English Printer,* Charles Knight.
7. Other instructions contained in the "Code of Chivalry" included: "respect and pity for all weakness and steadfastness in defending it"; "love of country"; "refusal to retreat before the enemy"; "loyalty to truth and the pledged word"; "generosity in giving"; "championship of the right and good in every place and at all times, against the forces of evil".
8. See *The Life of Mayster Wyllyam Caxton of the Weald of Kent,* the Rev. John Lewis.
9. *Ibid.*
10. See *Caxton & His World,* N. F. Blake.
11. *Ibid.*
12. *Ibid.*

CHAPTER 6

1. See *The Biography of William Caxton,* Blades.
2. For a full transcript of the proceedings of this law-suit see *The Biography of William Caxton,* Blades, revised edition by Frederick Muller, 1971.
3. See *The Complete Works of Sir Thomas More,* R. S. Silvester.
4. See *Mémoires,* Philippe de Commines.
5. See *A Book from Caxton's Library,* H. McCusker, in *More Books,* 6th series, XV (1940).

CHAPTER 7

1. See *A Short History of the Printed Word,* Warren Chappell, André Deutsch, 1972.

2. Cited by Charles Knight in *William Caxton: A Biography*. For further background on the Schoffers and Fust see also Warren Chappell's *A Short History of the Printed Word*.

3. *Typographical Antiquities*, the Rev. Dr. T. F. Dibdin.

4. Cited by Charles Knight in *William Caxton*.

5. *Ibid*.

6. See *A Dissertation concerning the origin of printing in England*, Conyers Middleton, 1735.

7. *Caxton & His World*, N. F. Blake.

8. *De Proprietatibus rerum* (Batholomeus Anglicus), printed by Wynkyn de Worde, 1495, Eng.

9. This work was presented to the Delegation of the Federation of Master Printers of Great Britain and Ireland on the occasion of their visit to the *Pressa* by the Langston Monotype Corporation, London.

10. See *William Caxton: An Essay*, Holbrook Jackson, William H. Robinson, London, 1933, limited edition of 100 copies.

11. See *Lettres d'un Bibliographie*, J. P. A. Madden. It should be pointed out that the Carthusians and the Crutched Friars as well as the Brothers of the Common Life had printing premises in Cologne.

12. See *William Caxton*, Charles Knight.

CHAPTER 8

1. See *The Golden Legend: The Legende of sayntes*, translation and version by Caxton, printed, 20 Nov., 1483.

2. Cited by Charles Knight in *William Caxton*.

3. See *William Caxton & His Critics*, by Curt F. Buhler.

4. See article entitled "William Caxton's Houses at Westminster" by Lawrence E. Tanner, Keeper of the Muniments, Westminster Abbey, in *The Library*, 5th series, Vol. XII, No. 3, Sept., 1957.

5. *Ibid*. A paper on this subject was read by Lawrence Tanner to the Bibliographical Society on 21 Feb., 1956.

6. *Ibid*. See also Westminster Abbey Muniments, 19736/7.

7. *Ibid*.

8. See *Phoenix of Fleet Street: 2000 Years of St. Brides*, Dewi Morgan, Knight.

9. "William Caxton's Houses at Westminster", *The Library*, Tanner.

10. See John Bagford's proposals for a life of Caxton, British Museum, Harley MS 5906, B. fo. 31. Bagford, referring to Caxton setting up a press in a house in the Almonry, stated: "and to this day the house is the sign of the King's Head; but to me it doth not seem so ancient, it being a brick building, which was very rare in those days." Samuel Palmer, in his *History of Printing*, comments that Bagford seems to have been unenterprising: "Mr. Bagford assigns the house in the Ambry which was formerly the King's Head, as the place where Caxton carried on his printing, but had I been early enough in my inquiry before twas

pulled down, as Mr. Bagford was, I flatter myself I could have found some remains. I have great reason to think it had been a printing-house, by having been inform'd that some persons found among the rubbish some remains of printing materials, but thro' ignorance of the curiosity of these, they are either lost or destroyed."

11. See *The Story of William Caxton*, Susan Cunnington.

12. See *William Caxton*, Henry R. Plomer.

13. See *William Caxton*, Edward Gordon Duff, privately printed, London, 1899.

14. See *William Caxton*, Plomer.

15. This quotation from Coplan is taken from the prologue to his own edition of *Kynge Apolyn of Thyre*. See also Blades.

16. An important source for a good deal of the information in this chapter is Walter J. B. Crotch: see his works *The Prologues and Epilogues of William Caxton*; an article, "Caxton on the Continent", *The Library*, 4th series vii (1926-7); "Caxton's Son-in-Law", *The Library*, ix (1928-1929).

CHAPTER 9

1. Cited in the *Westminster Abbey Official Guide*, Jarrold & Son, Norwich, 1971.

2. See *William Caxton*, Charles Knight.

3. *Polychronicon*, translated by Caxton from Trevisa's Latin version, 1482.

4. *Ibid.*

5. *William Caxton*, Plomer.

6. *Ibid.*

7. See *Scriptorum illustrium maioris Brytannie*, Bishop John Bale, Basle, 1557.

8. *William Caxton*, Plomer.

9. See also article entitled "William Caxton's Houses at Westminster" by Lawrence E. Tanner, *The Library*, 5th series, vol. xii, no. 3, Sept., 1957.

10. See *Charles the Great*, Caxton.

11. *William Caxton*, Plomer.

12. See *Caxton & His World*, Blake.

CHAPTER 10

1. See *William Caxton & His Critics*, Curt Buhler.

2. See *Eneydos*, Caxton, 1490.

3. *Ibid.*

4. See *Typographical Antiquities, or an Historical Account of the Origin & Progress of Printing in Great Britain & Ireland*, the Rev. Dr. Thomas F. Dibdin, 4 vols., 1810.

5. See *The Biography & Typography of William Caxton*, Blades.

6. See *Book of Fame*, by Geoffrey Chaucer, printed by Caxton, probably in 1484.

7. *Legenda Aurea—Legende Dorée—Golden Legend:* A study of Caxton's *Golden Legend* with special reference to its relations to the earlier English prose translation by Dr. Pierce Butler, John Hopkins University, Baltimore, 1899.

8. See *Caxton & His World*, Blake.

9. Game of Chess, translated from the French by Caxton, printed in Bruges, 1474.

10. *The Mirror of the World*, translated 1481, printed by Caxton. The origin of this work is not easily traceable and probably various sources were used, though an unknown writer of a Latin work, *Speculum vel Imago Mundi*, in the early 13th century must have supplied the original manuscript which was translated into French for the Duke of Berry in 1245. There was also a later translation which was most likely to have been used extensively by Caxton. The probability is that this work was heavily financed by Alderman Hugh Brice, of the City of London, especially as wood-engraving was used so freely and the intention of this patronage was for a book to be presented to Lord Hastings.

11. *Reynard the Fox*, translated from the Dutch by Caxton, printed 1481.

CHAPTER 11

1. See *The History of English Poetry*, Thomas Warton, London, 1778.

2. This is the first book advertisement in history and it contains the first mention of the Red Pale as being the sign of Caxton's printing-shop. The actual word used by Caxton for "Red" was "Reed". See also Blades' *William Caxton*.

3. See "William Caxton's Houses at Westminster", *The Library*, Tanner.

4. *The History of King Henry VII*, Francis Bacon, edited by J. A. Spedding, R. L. Ellis, D. D. Heath.

5. *Ibid.*

6. See W. J. B. Crotch.

7. See *William Caxton*, Charles Knight.

8. See Blades' *William Caxton*.

CHAPTER 12

1. *William Caxton*, Plomer.

2. For further details of Wynkyn de Worde's life see *Wynkyn de Worde*, James Moran, Wynkyn de Worde Society, London, 1960.

3. It has sometimes been suggested that both Treveris and William Machlinia worked for Caxton in his later years. This is possible, though it would probably be more accurate to say there was a degree of co-operation between them. When Caxton was faced with competition he always seemed to avoid confrontation and to seek collaboration instead.

4. John Rastell was the first man in England to publish a book containing music in which notes and horizontal stave lines were printed at one impression. Before Rastell's book lines and notes were printed separately. This book, printed about 1516, was entitled *A New Interlude and a Mery on the Nature of the iiij Elements*.

5. See *Wardrobe Accounts of Edward IV*, Sir Nicolas Harris Nicolas.

6. The *Penny Cyclopaedia* developed out of the *Penny Magazine* and soon showed

how the cheapest book of reference could still be the best. In the latter part of the eighteenth century the book-club came into being, one of the earliest, surprisingly enough, being launched by the poet, Robert Burns, who founded a society known as the Bachelors' Club. By the 1820's the book-club was beginning to prosper and Charles Knight's firm, in an effort to meet the principle of association in forming libraries or book-clubs among the people, issued a plan for the publication of *Knight's Weekly Volume for All Readers*, stating that "The friends of popular instruction—the people generally—feel that the rapidly growing appetite for information has not yet been adequately supplied. There is a demand for books of standard value and universal interest, cheap enough to find their way into every cottage, so trustworthy in facts, sound in their principles, and attractive in their subjects and their treatment, as to be welcome to the most instructed readers." Book-clubs and country lending libraries developed out of this plan.

7. See *Typographical Antiquities*, Ames & Herbert, revised edition, with notes by Dr. T. F. Dibdin, London, 1810.

Bibliography

AMES, Joseph & HERBERT, William: *Typographical Antiquities, or an Historical Account of the Origin and Progress of Printing in Great Britain and Ireland*, 3 vols. 1785. See also revised edition of 1810, with note by the Rev. Thomas Frognall Dibdin.

ATKINS, John W. H.: *English Literary Criticism: The Medieval Phase*, Cambridge University Press, 1943.

BENNETT, Henry S.: *The Pastons & Their England*, Cambridge University Press, 1922;
Caxton and his Public, an article in *The Review of English Studies*, xix, 1943.

BLADES, Rowland Hill: *Who Was Caxton?*, a monograph in *The Library*, 2nd. series, iv, 1902–3.

BLADES, William: *The Biography and Typography of William Caxton*, Trubner & Co., London, 1877. See also special edition of this book, published by Frederick Muller, London, in 1971, with introduction by James Moran.

BLAKE, Norman F.: *Caxton and His World*, André Deutsch, London, 1969;
Essay entitled *Caxton and the Courtly Style*, appearing *Essays & Studies*, collected for the English Association by Simeon Potter, John Murray, London, 1968.

BUHLER, Curt F.: *William Caxton and his Critics*, Syracuse University Press, 1959.

CALMETTE, Joseph: *The Golden Age of Burgundy: The Magnificent Dukes and their Court*, trans. by D. Weightman, Weidenfeld & Nicolson, London, 1962.

CHAPPELL, Warren: *A Short History of the Printed Word*, André Deutsch, London, 1972.

COLLISON, Robert L.: *Book Collecting: An Introduction to Modern Methods of Literary & Bibliographical Detection*, Ernest Benn, London, 1957.

CROTCH, Walter J. B.: *The Prologues and Epilogues of William Caxton*, EETS o.s. 176, Oxford University Press, London, 1928;
Caxton on the Continent, an article in *The Library*, 4th. series, vii, 1926–7;
Caxton's Son-in-Law, an article in *The Library*, ix, 1928–9.

CUNNINGTON, Susan: *The Story of William Caxton*, Harrap, London, 1917.

DUFF, Edward Gordon: *William Caxton*, Caxton Club, Chicago, 1905.

ELTON, G. R.: *Renaissance & Reformation*: 1300–1684, the Macmillan Company, New York, 1963.

FENN, Sir John: *Paston Letters: Original Letters written during the reigns of Henry VI, Edward IV and Richard III*, 2 vols., 1840.

FRANCIS, F. C.: *Robert Copland, Sixteenth Century Printer and Translator*, Jackson, Glasgow, 1961.

HAY, Denys: *Europe in the Fourteenth & Fifteenth Centuries*, Longmans, London, 1966.

JACKSON, Holbrook: *William Caxton: An Essay*, William H. Robinson, London, 1933.

JACKSON, John: *A Treatise on Wood-Engraving, Historical and Practical*, with illustrations engraved on wood, 1839.

KNIGHT, Charles: *William Caxton: First English Printer, A Biography*, Charles Knight & Co., London, 1844.

LEWIS, the Rev. John: *The Life of Mayster Wyllyam Caxton of the Weald of Kent*, London, 1737.

MADDEN, J. P. A.: *Lettres d'un Bibliographe*, Paris & Versailles, 1868–78.

MAITLAND, Thomas: *The History of London*, 2 vols., 1756.

MIDDLETON, Conyers: *A Dissertation concerning the origin of Printing in England*, 1735.

MORAN, James: *Wynkyn de Worde*, the Wynkyn de Worde Society, London, 1960.

MORGAN, Dewi: *Phoenix of Fleet Street: 2,000 Years of St. Brides*, Knight, London, 1974.

NICOLAS, Sir Nicolas Harris: *Wardrobe Accounts of Edward the Fourth*, 1830.

PLOMER, Henry R.: *William Caxton*, Leonard Parsons, London, 1925.

RICCI, Seymour de: *A Census of Caxtons*, Bibliographical Society, London, 1909.

ROBERTS, W. W.: *William Caxton, Writer and Critic*, Bulletin of the John Rylands Library, xiv, 1930.

ROWSE, A. L.: *Bosworth Field & The Wars of the Roses*, Macmillan, London, 1966.

SANDS, D. B.: *Caxton as a Literary Critic*, Papers of the Bibliographical Society of America, ii, 1957.

SCOFIELD, Cora: *The Life and Reign of Edward IV*, 2 vols., Longmans, London, 1923.

SKEAT, T. C.: *The Caxton Deeds*, article in the *British Museum Quarterly*, xxviii, 1964.

STOW, John: *Survey of the Cities of London & Westminster*, augmented by John Strype, 2 vols., 1720.

TANNER, Lawrence E.: *William Caxton's Houses at Westminster*, article in *The Library*, 5th. series, vol. xii, no. 3, Sept., 1957.

THOMAS, Henry: *Wilh. Caxton uyss Engelant, Evidence that the first English Printer learned his craft at Cologne*, privately printed at Cologne, 1928.

THRUPP, Sylvia L.: *The Merchant Class of Medieval London, 1300–1500*, University Press, Chicago, 1949.

TREVELYAN, G. M.: *English Social History: A Survey of Six Centuries*, Longmans, London, 1944.

VAUGHAN, Richard: *John the Fearless: the Growth of Burgundian Power*, Longmans, London, 1966.

WARTON, Thomas: *History of English Poetry*, 4 vols., 1824.

WELLS, James: *William Caxton*, Caxton Book Club, Chicago, 1960.

WINSHIP, George P.: *William Caxton and his Work*, University of California Press, 1937.

Also consulted:

The Westminster Abbey Muniments; *Documents inédits sur les enlumineurs de Bruges*, Le Beffroi, iv, 1872–3; the Churchwardens' Accounts of St. Margaret's, Westminster; the British Museum; the Almoner's Account Rolls, Westminster Abbey; *Caxton and the Early Printers*, by Sylvie Nickels in the Jackdaw Publications Series; Extracts from the Issue Rolls of the Exchequer, Henry III to Henry VI, 1837; the Guildhall Library, London; the Public Record Office, London.

Acknowledgements

The author wishes to express his thanks and acknowledge the help he has received from the Librarian and his staff at Westminster Abbey, the British Museum and Public Record Office; from Mr. James Moran, a leading authority on the typography of Caxton; from Mr. Nigel Nicolson for helping to track down the origin of some legends about Caxton. He also gratefully acknowledges permission from Professor N. F. Blake, of the University of Sheffield, to use quotations from his work *Caxton & His World*, André Deutsch, London, and his Essay on *Caxton and the Courtly Style* appearing in *Essays & Studies*, John Murray, London.

Index